Articles of Agreement

This Agreement is made the _____ 20 _____

Between

The Employer _____

_____

_____ (Company No._____)[1]

of/whose registered office is at _____

_____

_____

And

The Contractor _____

_____

_____(Company No. _____)[1]

of/whose registered office is at _____

_____

_____

[1]   Where the Employer or Contractor is neither a company incorporated under the Companies Acts nor a company registered under the laws of another country, delete the references to Company number and registered office. In the case of a company incorporated outside England and Wales, particulars of its place of incorporation should be inserted immediately before its Company number. As to execution by foreign companies and matters of jurisdiction, see the Design and Build Contract Guide.

Whereas

First the Employer wishes to have the design and construction of the following work carried out[2]:

_____

_____

at _____

_____ ('the Works')

and the Employer has supplied to the Contractor documents showing and describing or otherwise stating his requirements ('the Employer's Requirements');

Second in response to the Employer's Requirements the Contractor has supplied to the Employer:

- documents showing and describing the Contractor's proposals for the design and construction of the Works ('the Contractor's Proposals'); and

- an analysis of the Contract Sum ('the Contract Sum Analysis');

Third the Employer has examined the Contractor's Proposals and, subject to the Conditions, is satisfied that they appear to meet the Employer's Requirements[3];

Fourth for the purposes of the Construction Industry Scheme (CIS) under the Finance Act 2004, the status of the Employer is, as at the Base Date, that stated in the Contract Particulars;

Fifth the division of the Works into Sections is shown in the Employer's Requirements or in such other documents as are identified in the Contract Particulars[4];

Sixth where so stated in the Contract Particulars, this Contract is supplemented by the Framework Agreement identified in those particulars;

Seventh the Supplemental Provisions identified in the Contract Particulars apply;

---

[2] State nature and location of intended works.

[3] Where the Employer has accepted a divergence from his requirements in the proposals submitted by the Contractor, the divergence should be removed by amending the Employer's Requirements before the Contract is executed.

[4] Delete the Fifth Recital if the Works are not divided into Sections.

Now it is hereby agreed as follows

Article 1: Contractor's obligations

The Contractor shall complete the design for the Works and carry out and complete the construction of the Works in accordance with the Contract Documents.

Article 2: Contract Sum

The Employer shall pay the Contractor at the times and in the manner specified in the Conditions the VAT-exclusive sum of

_____

_____ (£ _____._____) ('the Contract Sum')

or such other sum as shall become payable under this Contract.

Article 3: Employer's Agent

For the purposes of this Contract the Employer's Agent is

_____

of _____

_____

or such other person as the Employer shall nominate in his place. Save to the extent that the Employer may otherwise specify by notice to the Contractor, the Employer's Agent shall have full authority to receive and issue applications, consents, instructions, notices, requests or statements and otherwise to act for the Employer under any of the Conditions.

Article 4: Employer's Requirements and Contractor's Proposals

The Employer's Requirements, the Contractor's Proposals and the Contract Sum Analysis are those referred to in the Contract Particulars.

Article 5: CDM Co-ordinator

The CDM Co-ordinator for the purposes of the CDM Regulations is the Contractor

(or)[5] _____

---

[5]   Insert the name of the CDM Co-ordinator only where the Contractor is not to fulfil that role, and that of the Principal Contractor only if that is to be a person other than the Contractor. If the project is not notifiable under the CDM Regulations 2007 (i.e. a project which is not likely to involve more than 30 days, or 500 person days, of construction work or which is being carried out for a homeowner as a purely domestic project), delete Articles 5 and 6 in their entirety.

of _____

_____

or, if he ceases to be the CDM Co-ordinator, such other person as the Employer shall appoint pursuant to regulation 14(~~34~~) of those regulations.

Article 6: Principal Contractor

The Principal Contractor for the purposes of the CDM Regulations and the SWMP Regulations is the Contractor

(or)[5] _____

of _____

_____

or, if he ceases to be the Principal Contractor, such other contractor as the Employer shall appoint pursuant to regulation 14(~~32~~) of the CDM Regulations and/or regulation 4 of the SWMP Regulations ~~those regulations~~.

Article 7: Adjudication

If any dispute or difference arises under this Contract, either Party may refer it to adjudication in accordance with clause 9·2[6].

Article 8: Arbitration

Where Article 8 applies[7], then, subject to Article 7 and the exceptions set out below, any dispute or difference between the Parties of any kind whatsoever arising out of or in connection with this Contract shall be referred to arbitration in accordance with clauses 9·3 to 9·8 and the JCT ~~2005~~ 2011 edition of the Construction Industry Model Arbitration Rules (CIMAR). The exceptions to this Article 8 are:

- any disputes or differences arising under or in respect of the Construction Industry Scheme or VAT, to the extent that legislation provides another method of resolving such disputes or differences; and

- any disputes or differences in connection with the enforcement of any decision of an Adjudicator.

Article 9: Legal proceedings[7]

Subject to Article 7 and (where it applies) to Article 8, the English courts shall have jurisdiction over any dispute or difference between the Parties which arises out of or in connection with this Contract.

---

[6]   As to adjudication in cases where the Employer is a residential occupier within the meaning of section 106 of the Housing Grants, Construction and Regeneration Act 1996, see the Design and Build Contract Guide.

[7]   If it is intended, subject to the right of adjudication and exceptions stated in Article 8, that disputes or differences should be determined by arbitration and not by legal proceedings, the Contract Particulars **must** state that Article 8 and clauses 9·3 to 9·8 apply and the words "do not apply" **must** be deleted. If the Parties wish any dispute or difference to be determined by the courts of another jurisdiction the appropriate amendment should be made to Article 9 (see also clause 1·10 and Schedule 5 Parts 1 and 2).

Contract Particulars

*Note: An asterisk * indicates text that is to be deleted as appropriate.*

Part 1: General

Clause etc.	*Subject*	
Fourth Recital and clause 4·5	Construction Industry Scheme (CIS)	Employer at the Base Date * is a 'contractor'/is not a 'contractor' for the purposes of the CIS
Fifth Recital	Description of Sections (if any) *(If not shown or described in the Employer's Requirements, state the reference numbers and dates or other identifiers of documents in which they are shown.)*[8]	_____ _____ _____ _____
Sixth Recital	Framework Agreement (if applicable) *(State date, title and parties.)*	_____ _____ _____ _____
Seventh Recital and Part 1 of Schedule 2	Supplemental Provisions – Part 1 *(Where neither entry against an item below is deleted, the relevant paragraph does not apply.)*	
	Site Manager	Paragraph 1 * applies/does not apply
	Named Sub-Contractors	Paragraph 2 * applies/does not apply
	Bills of Quantities	Paragraph 3 * applies/does not apply
	Valuation of Changes – Contractor's estimates	Paragraph 4 * applies/does not apply
	Loss and expense – Contractor's estimates	Paragraph 5 * applies/does not apply

[8]   If the relevant document or set of documents takes the form of an Annex to this Contract, it is sufficient to refer to that Annex.

Seventh Recital and Part 2 of Schedule 2	**Supplemental Provisions – Part 2** *(Where neither entry against an item below is deleted, the relevant paragraph applies.)*	
	Acceleration Quotation	Paragraph 6 * applies/does not apply
	Collaborative working	Paragraph 7 * applies/does not apply
	Health and safety	Paragraph 8 * applies/does not apply
	Cost savings and value improvements	Paragraph 9 * applies/does not apply
	Sustainable development and environmental considerations	Paragraph 10 * applies/does not apply
	Performance Indicators and monitoring	Paragraph 11 * applies/does not apply
	Notification and negotiation of disputes	Paragraph 12 * applies/does not apply
	Where paragraph 12 applies, the respective nominees of the Parties are	Employer's nominee _____ _____ Contractor's nominee _____ _____ or such replacement as each Party may notify to the other from time to time
Article 4	**Employer's Requirements** *(State reference numbers and dates or other identifiers of documents in which these are contained.)*[8]	_____ _____ _____ _____
Article 4	**Contractor's Proposals** *(State reference numbers and dates or other identifiers of documents in which these are contained.)*[8]	_____ _____ _____ _____

Article 4	Contract Sum Analysis *(State reference numbers and dates or other identifiers of documents in which this is contained.)*[8]	_____ _____ _____ _____

Article 8	Arbitration *(If neither entry is deleted, Article 8 and clauses 9·3 to 9·8 do not apply. If disputes and differences are to be determined by arbitration and not by legal proceedings, it <u>must</u> be stated that Article 8 and clauses 9·3 to 9·8 apply.)*[9]	Article 8 and clauses 9·3 to 9·8 *(Arbitration)* * apply/do not apply

1·1	Base Date	_____

1·1	CDM Planning Period[10]	shall mean the period of _____ * days/weeks * ending on the Date of Possession/ * beginning/ending on _____ 20 _____

1·1	Date for Completion of the Works *(where completion by Sections does not apply)* Sections: Dates for Completion of Sections[11]	_____ Section _____ : _____ Section _____ : _____ Section _____ : _____

1·7	Addresses for service of notices by the Parties *(If none is stated, the address in each case, subject to clause 1·7·3, shall be that shown at the commencement of the Agreement.)*[12]	Employer _____ _____ _____ Contractor _____ _____ _____

---

[9]   On factors to be taken into account by the Parties in considering whether disputes are to be determined by arbitration or by legal proceedings, see the Design and Build Contract Guide. See also footnote [7].

[10]   Under the CDM Regulations 2007 every client is expressly required to allocate sufficient time (the CDM Planning Period) prior to the commencement of construction to enable contractors and others to carry out necessary CDM planning and preparation. There may be cases where that planning and preparation needs to be completed earlier than the Date of Possession and adaptation of the entries may be needed where there are Sections.

[11]   Continue on further sheets if necessary, which should be signed or initialled by or on behalf of each Party and then be annexed to this Contract.

[12]   As to service of notices etc. outside the United Kingdom, see the Design and Build Contract Guide.

2·3	Date of Possession of the site *(where possession by Sections does not apply)*	_____ 20_____
	Sections: Dates of Possession of Sections[11]	Section _____ : _____ 20_____
		Section _____ : _____ 20_____
		Section _____ : _____ 20_____

2·4	Deferment of possession of the site *(where possession by Sections does not apply)*	Clause 2·4 * applies/does not apply
		Maximum period of deferment (if less than 6 weeks) is
		_____
	Sections: deferment of possession of Sections	Clause 2·4 * applies/does not apply
		Maximum period of deferment (if less than 6 weeks) is[11]
		Section _____ : _____
		Section _____ : _____
		Section _____ : _____

| 2·17·3 | Limit of Contractor's liability for loss of use etc. (if any) | £ _____ |

2·29·2	Liquidated damages *(where completion by Sections does not apply)*	at the rate of
		£ _____ per _____
	Sections: rate of liquidated damages for each Section[11]	Section _____ : £ _____ per _____
		Section _____ : £ _____ per _____
		Section _____ : £ _____ per _____

2·34	Sections: Section Sums[11]	Section _____ : £ _____
		Section _____ : £ _____
		Section _____ : £ _____

2·35	Rectification Period *(where completion by Sections does not apply)* *(If no other period is stated, the period is 6 months.)*	_____ months from the date of practical completion of the Works
	Sections: Rectification Periods[11] *(If no other period is stated, the period is 6 months.)*	Section _____ : _____ months
		Section _____ : _____ months
		Section _____ : _____ months from the date of practical completion of each Section

4·6	Advance payment *(Not applicable where the Employer is a Local Authority)*	Clause 4·6 * applies/does not apply If applicable: the advance payment will be[13] £ _____ / _____ per cent of the Contract Sum and will be paid to the Contractor on _____ ; it will be reimbursed to the Employer in the following amount(s) and at the following time(s) _____ _____ _____ _____
4·6	Advance Payment Bond *(Not applicable where the Employer is a Local Authority)* *(Where an advance payment is to be made, an advance payment bond is required unless stated that it is not required.)*	An advance payment bond * is/is not required
4·7	Method of payment – alternatives[14] *(If no Alternative is selected, Alternative B applies.)*	* by stages in accordance with Alternative A (clause 4·13)/ * periodically in accordance with Alternative B (clause 4·14)
	Alternative A: Stage Payments	The stages referred to in clause 4·8·2 4·9·1 are ~~as follows/ set out on a separate sheet attached:~~ * set out in the following document[8] _____ _____ _____ _____ / * as follows:
	Stages (insert brief description) _____	Cumulative value £ _____

[13] Insert either a monetary amount or a percentage figure, delete the alternative and complete the other required details.

[14] Delete whichever Alternative is not applicable. Where Interim Payments are to be made by stages (including by quantity of units and sub-units completed) make the appropriate entries or prepare and insert a separate schedule of cumulative stage values ~~on a separate sheet~~.

	£ _____
_____	£ _____
_____	£ _____
_____	£ _____
_____	£ _____
_____	£ _____
_____	£ _____
_____	£ _____
_____	[15] £ _____

	Alternative B: Periodic Payments – Dates of Interim Applications ~~for Interim Payment~~ *(If no date ~~none~~ is stated, the date for the first Interim* Application ~~Payment~~ *is ~~to be made within~~ one month* after ~~of~~ *the Date of Possession.)*	The first date is: _____ and thereafter the same date in each month or the nearest Business Day in that month[16]
4·15·4	Listed Items – uniquely identified *(Delete the entry if no bond is required.)*	* For uniquely identified Listed Items a bond in respect of payment for such items is required for £ _____
4·15·5	Listed Items – not uniquely identified *(Delete the entry if clause 4·15·5 does not apply.)*	* For Listed Items that are not uniquely identified a bond in respect of payment for such items is required for £ _____
4·17	Contractor's Retention Bond *(Not applicable where the Employer is a Local Authority)* *(Not applicable unless stated to apply and relevant particulars are given below)*	Clause 4·17 * applies/does not apply If clause 4·17 applies, the maximum aggregate sum for the purposes of clause 2 of the bond is £ _____ For the purposes of clause 6·3 of the bond, the expiry date shall be _____

---

[15]   Cumulative value of final stage must be equal to the Contract Sum.

[16]   The first date should not be more than one month after the Date of Possession. Where it is intended that Interim Applications ~~for Interim Payment~~ be made on the last day of each month, the entry may be completed/amended to read "the last day of *(insert month)* and thereafter the last day in each month or the nearest Business Day in that month." After practical completion, clause ~~4·8·3~~ 4·9·2 provides for intervals of 2 months (or such other period as the Parties agree) between Interim Applications ~~for Interim Payment~~.

4·18·1	Retention Percentage *(The percentage is 3 per cent unless a* *different rate is stated; if no retention is* *required, insert 'Nil' or '0'.)*	_____ per cent

4·19 and Schedule 7	Fluctuations Options[17] *(If no Fluctuations Option is selected, Option A* *applies.)*	Schedule 7: * Fluctuations Option A applies/ * Fluctuations Option B applies/ * Fluctuations Option C applies
	Percentage addition for Fluctuations Option A, paragraph A·12 or Option B, paragraph B·13	_____ per cent
	Formula Rules for Fluctuations Option C, paragraph C·1·2	Rule 3: Base Month _____ 20_____
	(For Local Authorities only)	Rule 3: Non-Adjustable Element _____ per cent
	(Unless Part II is stated to apply, Part I *applies.)*	Rules 10 and 30(i): * Part I/Part II of section 2 of the Formula Rules applies[18]

5·5	Daywork	The Percentage Additions to each section of the prime cost or, if they apply in respect of labour, the All-Inclusive Rates, are set out in the following document[8] _____ _____ _____ _____

6·4·1·2	Contractor's insurance: injury to persons or property – insurance cover *(for any one* *occurrence or series of occurrences arising out* *of one event)*	£ _____

6·5·1	Insurance – liability of Employer	Minimum amount of indemnity for any one occurrence or series of occurrences arising out of one event £ _____ [19]

---

[17]   Delete all but one.

[18]   The Part to be deleted depends upon which method of formula adjustment (Part I – Work Category Method or Part II – Work Group
Method) is applicable.

[19]   Insert an amount where it is stated in the Employer's Requirements that insurance under clause 6·5·1 is required. If the indemnity is
to be for an aggregate amount and not for any one occurrence or series of occurrences the entry should be amended to make this
clear.

6·7 and Schedule 3	Insurance of the Works – Insurance Options[17][20]	Schedule 3: * Insurance Option A applies/ * Insurance Option B applies/ * Insurance Option C applies
6·7 and Schedule 3 Insurance Option A (paragraphs A·1 and A·3), B (paragraph B·1) or C (paragraph C·2)	Percentage to cover professional fees *(If no other percentage is stated, it shall be 15 per cent.)*	_____ per cent
6·7 and Schedule 3 Insurance Option A (paragraph A·3)	Annual renewal date of insurance *(as supplied by the Contractor)*	_____
6·10 and Schedule 3	Terrorism Cover – details of the required cover *(State reference numbers and dates or other identifiers of documents setting out the requirements. Unless otherwise stated, Pool Re Cover is required.)*	_____ _____ _____
6·12~~11~~	Professional Indemnity insurance	
	Level of cover *(If an alternative is not selected the amount shall be the aggregate amount for any one period of insurance. A period of insurance for these purposes shall be one year unless otherwise stated.)* *(If no amount is stated, insurance under clause 6·12~~11~~ shall not be required.)*	Amount of indemnity required * relates to claims or series of claims arising out of one event/ * is the aggregate amount for any one period of insurance and is £ _____
	~~Sub-limits within the overall level of cover~~	
	Cover for pollution and contamination claims *(If no amount is stated, such cover shall not be required; unless otherwise stated, the required limit of indemnity is an annual aggregate amount.)*	* is required, with a sub-limit of indemnity of £ _____ / * is not required
	~~Cover for asbestos claims~~ ~~*(If no amount is stated, such cover shall not be required; unless otherwise stated, the required limit of indemnity is an annual aggregate amount.)*~~	*~~is required, with a limit of indemnity of~~ ~~£ _____ /~~ *~~is not required~~
	~~Cover for fungal mould claims~~	*~~is required/~~ *~~is not required~~

[20]   Obtaining Terrorism Cover, which is necessary in order to comply with the requirements of Insurance Option A, B or C, will involve an additional premium and may in certain situations be difficult to effect. Where a difficulty arises discussion should take place between the Parties and their insurance advisers. See the Design and Build Contract Guide.

	Expiry of required period of Professional Indemnity insurance is *(If no period is selected, the expiry date shall be 6 years from the date of practical completion of the Works.)*	* 6 years/ * 12 years/ * _____ years (not exceeding 12 years)
6·14~~13~~	Joint Fire Code	The Joint Fire Code * applies/does not apply[21]
	If the Joint Fire Code applies, state whether the insurer under Schedule 3, Insurance Option A, B or C (paragraph C·2) has specified that the Works are a 'Large Project':	* Yes/No[21]
6·17~~16~~	Joint Fire Code – amendments/revisions *(The cost shall be borne by the Contractor unless otherwise stated.)*	The cost, if any, of compliance with amendment(s) or revision(s) to the Joint Fire Code shall be borne by * the Employer/the Contractor
7·2	Assignment/grant by Employer of rights under clause 7·2 *(If neither entry is deleted, clause 7·2 applies.)*	Clause 7·2 * applies/does not apply
	Sections: rights under clause 7·2 *(If clause 7·2 applies, amend the entry if rights under that clause are to apply to certain Sections only.)*	* Rights under clause 7·2 apply to each Section
8·9·2	Period of suspension *(If none is stated, the period is 2 months.)*	_____
8·11·1·1 to 8·11·1·6	Period of suspension *(If none is stated, the period is 2 months.)*	_____
9·2·1	Adjudication[22]	The Adjudicator is _____
	Nominating body – where no Adjudicator is named or where the named Adjudicator is unwilling or unable to act (whenever that is established)[23] *(Where an Adjudicator is not named and a nominating body has not been selected, the nominating body shall be one of the bodies listed opposite selected by the Party requiring the reference to adjudication.)*	* Royal Institute of British Architects * The Royal Institution of Chartered Surveyors * constructionadjudicators.com[24] * ~~Construction Confederation~~ Association of Independent Construction * Adjudicators[25] ~~National Specialist Contractors Council~~ Chartered Institute of Arbitrators

---

9·4·1 Arbitration[26] – appointor of Arbitrator (and of any replacement)[27]
(If no appointor is selected, the appointor shall be the President or a Vice-President of the Royal Institute of British Architects.)

President or a Vice-President:
* Royal Institute of British Architects
* The Royal Institution of Chartered Surveyors
* Chartered Institute of Arbitrators

---

[26] This only applies where the Contract Particulars state (against the reference to Article 8) that Article 8 and clauses 9·3 to 9·8 (*Arbitration*) apply.

[27] Delete all but one of the bodies asterisked.

Part 2: Third Party Rights and Collateral Warranties

If such rights or warranties are required from the Contractor, complete the particulars in (A) to (D) below:

P&T Rights Particulars

(A) **Identity of Purchasers/Tenants on whom P&T Rights may be conferred, and whether (in the case of the Contractor) those rights are to be conferred as third party rights (clause 7A) or by Collateral Warranty (clause 7C)[28]**

Clauses 7A, 7C and 7E of the Conditions	Name, class or description of person[29]	The part of the Works to be purchased or let	State in each case which of clause 7A or 7C applies
	_____	_____	_____

(P&T Rights are conferred only on persons who are sufficiently identified in the first column. If in relation to an identified person it is not stated whether P&T Rights from the Contractor are to be conferred under clause 7A (Third Party Rights) or under clause 7C (Collateral Warranty CWa/P&T), clause 7A shall apply.)

---

[28]   The Contractor may be required to grant rights either as Third Party Rights or Collateral Warranties. In the case of sub-contractors, provision is made only for the grant of Collateral Warranties – see Part 2(E) of these particulars and the Design and Build Contract Guide.

[29]   As to the Contracts (Rights of Third Parties) Act 1999 and identification of beneficiaries, see the Design and Build Contract Guide.

Paragraph of Schedule 5, Part 1 or Clause of CWa/P&T[30]	**(B) P&T Rights from the Contractor**	
1·1·2	Applicability of paragraph/clause 1·1·2	Paragraph/clause 1·1·2[30] * applies/does not apply
	Maximum liability *(Unless paragraph/clause 1·1·2 is stated to apply <u>and</u> the maximum liability is stated, paragraph/clause 1·1·2 does not apply.)*	The maximum liability is £ _____
	Type of maximum liability *(If not stated, it shall be an aggregate limit on liability.)*	* Maximum liability is in respect of each breach/ * Maximum liability is an aggregate limit on liability

Funder Rights Particulars

Clauses 7B, 7D and 7E of the Conditions	**(C) Identity of Funder in whom Funder Rights may be vested under this Contract** *(If not identified by name, class or description, Funder Rights shall not be required from the Contractor.)*	_____ _____
Paragraph of Schedule 5, Part 2 or Clause of CWa/F[30]	**(D) Funder Rights from the Contractor** Nature of Funder Rights from the Contractor *(If neither clause reference is deleted, clause 7B applies.)*	* Clause 7B (Third Party Rights) applies/ * Clause 7D (Collateral Warranty) applies

---

[30]   The paragraph numbers in Schedule 5 are the same as the clause numbers in the JCT Collateral Warranty.

Collateral Warranties from Sub-Contractors

(E) If warranties are required from sub-contractors, complete the particulars below:

Clauses 3·3 and 3·4 of the Conditions	Sub-contractors from whom Warranties may be required[31]	Type(s) of warranty (SCWa/P&T, SCWa/F, SCWa/E) required [32] from each sub-contractor	Levels of Professional Indemnity insurance required (if applicable)[33]

For these purposes, unless otherwise stated:

(i)   all Purchasers and Tenants identified at (A) above, any Funder identified at (C) above and the Employer shall be entitled to a warranty from a sub-contractor where the appropriate type is shown above as required from him;

(ii)   **if applicable, the levels of Professional Indemnity insurance must be specified**[33]; the basis of that cover shall be whichever applies under the Contract Particulars for clause 6·1244;

(iii)   if a maximum liability is specified under (B) above, that shall also apply in relation to all sub-contractors' Collateral Warranties unless a lower amount is specified.

---

[31]   Employers should be selective in listing the sub-contractors (or categories of sub-contractor) including any consultants from whom collateral warranties may be required (see the Design and Build Contract Guide).

[32]   Where a sub-contractor is required to grant Collateral Warranties of the types referred to in clause 7E (i.e. the Sub-Contractor Collateral Warranty for a Purchaser or Tenant (SCWa/P&T), for a Funder (SCWa/F) and for the Employer (SCWa/E)), state the particular type(s). All three Collateral Warranties are documents prepared by JCT.

[33]   Professional Indemnity insurance applies only where the sub-contractor has design responsibilities. As to cover levels, see the Design and Build Contract Guide.

Note on Execution

This Agreement should be executed by both the Employer and the Contractor either under hand or as a deed. As to factors relevant to that choice, see the Design and Build Contract Guide.

Execution under hand

If this Agreement is to be executed under hand, use the form set out on the following page. Each Party or his authorised representative should sign where indicated in the presence of a witness who should then sign and set out his name and address.

Execution as a Deed

If this Agreement is to be executed as a deed, each Party should use the relevant form marked 'Execution as a Deed' in accordance with the notes provided.

Other forms of Attestation

In cases where the forms of attestation set out are not appropriate, e.g. in the case of certain housing associations and partnerships or if a Party wishes an attorney to execute this Agreement on his behalf, the appropriate form(s) may be inserted in the vacant space opposite and/or below.

As witness

the hands of the Parties
or their duly authorised representatives

Signed by or on behalf of
the Employer

_____

in the presence of:

_____
witness' signature

_____
witness' name

_____
witness' address

_____

Signed by or on behalf of
the Contractor

_____

in the presence of:

_____
witness' signature

_____
witness' name

_____
witness' address

_____

Notes on Execution as a Deed

1. For the purposes of execution as a deed, two forms are provided for execution, one for the Employer and the other for the Contractor. Each form provides four methods of execution, **(A)** to **(D)**, for use as appropriate. The full name of the Employer or Contractor (whether an individual, a company or other body) should be inserted where indicated at the commencement of the relevant form. This applies irrespective of the method used.

2. For public and private companies incorporated and registered under the Companies Acts, the three principal methods of execution as a deed are:

   (A) through signature by a Director and the Company Secretary or by two Directors;

   (B) by affixing the company's common seal in the presence of a Director and the *Company* Secretary or of two Directors or other duly authorised officers; or

   (C) signature by a single Director in the presence of a witness who attests the signature.

   Methods **(A)** and **(C)** are available to public and private companies whether or not they have a common seal. (Method **(C)** was introduced by section 44(2)(b) of the Companies Act 2006.) Methods **(A)** and **(C)** are not available under companies legislation to local authorities or to certain other bodies corporate, e.g. bodies incorporated by letters patent or private Act of Parliament that are not registered under companies legislation and such bodies may only use method **(B)**.

3. Where method **(A)** is being used, delete the inappropriate words and insert in the spaces indicated the names of the two Directors, or of the Director and the Company Secretary, who are to sign.

4. If method **(B)** (affixing the common seal) is adopted in cases where either or both the authorised officers attesting its affixation are not themselves a Director or the *Company* Secretary, their respective office(s) should be substituted for the reference(s) to Director and/or to *Company* Secretary/Director. (In the case of execution by bodies that are not companies, the reference to "*Company*" under the second signature should be deleted where appropriate.)

5. Method **(C)** (execution by a single Director) has been introduced primarily, but not exclusively, for 'single officer' companies. The Director should sign where indicated in the presence of a witness who should then sign and set out his name and address.

6. Where the Employer or Contractor is an individual, he should use method **(D)** and sign where indicated in the presence of a witness who should then sign and set out his name and address.

Executed as a Deed by the Employer

namely [1] _____

(A) acting by a Director and the Company Secretary/two Directors **of the company** [2, 3]

_____ and _____
(Print name of signatory)   *(Print name of signatory)*

_____   _____
Signature   Director   *Signature*   Company Secretary/Director

(B) by affixing hereto the common seal **of the company/other body corporate** [2, 4]

in the presence of

_____
Signature   Director

_____
Signature   Company Secretary/Director   *[Common seal of company]*

(C) by attested signature of a single Director **of the company** [2, 5]

_____
Signature   Director

in the presence of

Witness' signature _____ *(Print name)* _____

Witness' address _____

(D) by attested signature **of the individual** [6]

_____
Signature

in the presence of

Witness' signature _____ *(Print name)* _____

Witness' address _____

Note: The numbers on this page refer to the numbered paragraphs in the Notes on Execution as a Deed.

Executed as a Deed by the Contractor

namely [1] _____

(A) acting by a Director and the Company Secretary/two Directors **of the company** [2, 3]

_____   and   _____
(Print name of signatory)   *(Print name of signatory)*

_____   _____
Signature   Director   *Signature*   Company Secretary/Director

(B) by affixing hereto the common seal **of the company/other body corporate** [2, 4]

in the presence of

_____
Signature   Director

_____
Signature   Company Secretary/Director   *[Common seal of company]*

(C) by attested signature of a single Director **of the company** [2, 5]

_____
Signature   Director

in the presence of

Witness' signature _____ *(Print name)* _____

Witness' address _____

(D) by attested signature **of the individual** [6]

_____
Signature

in the presence of

Witness' signature _____ *(Print name)* _____

Witness' address _____

Note: The numbers on this page refer to the numbered paragraphs in the Notes on Execution as a Deed.

Conditions

Section 1   Definitions and Interpretation

Definitions

1·1   Unless the context otherwise requires or the Agreement or these Conditions specifically provide otherwise, the following words and phrases, where they appear in capitalised form in the Agreement or these Conditions, shall have the meanings stated or referred to below:

Word or phrase	Meaning
Acceleration Quotation:	a quotation by the Contractor for an acceleration in the carrying out of the Works or a Section made under paragraph 6 of **Schedule 2**.
Adjudicator:	an individual appointed under **clause 9·2** as the Adjudicator.
Agreement:	the Articles of Agreement to which these Conditions are annexed, consisting of the Recitals, the Articles and the Contract Particulars.
All Risks Insurance:	see **clause 6·8**.
~~Applications for Interim Payment:~~	~~see clause 4·9.~~
Arbitrator:	an individual appointed under **clause 9·4** as the Arbitrator.
Article:	an article in the **Agreement**.
Base Date:	the date stated as such date in the **Contract Particulars** (against the reference to **clause 1·1**)[34].
Business Day:	any day which is not a Saturday, a Sunday or a Public Holiday.
CDM Co-ordinator:	the Contractor or other person named in **Article 5** or any successor appointed by the Employer.
CDM Planning Period:	the minimum amount of time referred to in regulation 10(2)(c) of the CDM Regulations, as specified in the **Contract Particulars** (against the reference to **clause 1·1**).
CDM Regulations:	the Construction (Design and Management) Regulations 2007.
Change:	see **clause 5·1**.
Completion Date:	the Date for Completion of the Works or of a Section as stated in the **Contract Particulars** or such other date as is fixed either under **clause 2·25** or by a Pre-agreed Adjustment.
Conditions:	the clauses set out in sections 1 to 9 of these Conditions, together with and including the Schedules hereto.

---

[34]   The Base Date is relevant (inter alia) to clause 2·15·2·1 (changes in Statutory Requirements) and the Fluctuations Options (Schedule 7) and it helps to determine the edition/issue and/or version of documents relevant to this Contract, e.g. definitions of the prime cost of daywork (clause 5·5).

Confirmed Acceptance:	the Employer's instruction confirming acceptance of an Acceleration Quotation under paragraph 6 of **Schedule 2**.
Construction Industry Scheme (or 'CIS'):	see the **Fourth Recital**.
Construction Phase Plan:	the plan prepared by the Principal Contractor, where the project is notifiable under the CDM Regulations and in order to comply with regulation 23, including any updates and revisions.
Contract Documents:	the Agreement and these Conditions, together with the Employer's Requirements, the Contractor's Proposals and the Contract Sum Analysis.
Contract Particulars:	the particulars in the **Agreement** and there described as such, including the entries made by the Parties.
Contract Sum:	the sum stated in **Article 2**.
Contract Sum Analysis:	see the **Second Recital** and the **Contract Particulars**.
Contractor:	the person named as Contractor in the **Agreement**.
Contractor's Design Documents:	the drawings, details and specifications of materials, goods and workmanship and other related documents prepared by or for the Contractor in relation to the design of the Works.
Contractor's Persons:	the Contractor's employees and agents, all other persons employed or engaged on or in connection with the Works or any part of them and any other person properly on the site in connection therewith, excluding the Employer, Employer's Persons and any Statutory Undertaker.
Contractor's Proposals:	see the **Second Recital** and the **Contract Particulars**.
Date for Completion:	the date stated as such date in the **Contract Particulars** (against the reference to **clause 1·1**) in relation to the Works or a Section.
Date of Possession:	the date stated as such date in the **Contract Particulars** (against the reference to **clause 2·3**) in relation to the Works or a Section.
Development Control Requirements:	any statutory provisions and any decision of a relevant authority thereunder which control the right to develop the site.
Employer:	the person named as Employer in the **Agreement**.
Employer's Agent:	see **Article 3**.
Employer's Final Statement:	the final statement prepared by or on behalf of the Employer pursuant to **clause 4·12·4**.
Employer's Persons:	all persons employed, engaged or authorised by the Employer, excluding the Contractor, Contractor's Persons, and any Statutory Undertaker but including any such third party as is referred to in clause 3·15·2.
Employer's Requirements:	see the **First Recital** and the **Contract Particulars**.
Excepted Risks:	see **clause 6·8**.
Final Statement:	see **clauses 1·8** and **4·12**.
Finance Agreement:	the agreement between the Funder and the Employer for the provision of finance for the Works.
Fluctuations Options A, B and C:	the provisions set out in **Schedule 7** (see **clause 4·19** and the **Contract Particulars**).

Funder:	the person named or otherwise sufficiently identified as such in or by the Funder Rights Particulars and in respect of whom the Employer gives notice under **clause 7B·1**.
Funder Rights:	the rights in favour of the Funder set out in **Part 2 of Schedule 5** or in the appropriate form of collateral warranty.
Funder Rights Particulars:	the entries against **clause 6·12~~11~~** in **Part 1** and the relevant items and entries in that section of **Part 2 of the Contract Particulars**.
Gross Valuation:	see **clauses 4·13** and **4·14**.
Insolvent:	see **clause 8·1**.
Insurance Options A, B and C:	the provisions relating to insurance of the Works and (where applicable) existing structures set out in **Schedule 3**.
Interest Rate:	a rate 5% per annum above the official dealing rate of the Bank of England current at the date that a payment due under this Contract becomes overdue.
Interim Application:	see **clause 4·8**.
Interim Payment:	any of the payments to which **clause 4·7** and the **Contract Particulars** refer.
Joint Fire Code:	the Joint Code of Practice on the Protection from Fire of Construction Sites and Buildings Undergoing Renovation, published by the Construction Confederation and the Fire Protection Association, current at the Base Date.
Joint Names Policy:	see **clause 6·8**.
Listed Items:	materials, goods and/or items prefabricated for inclusion in the Works which are listed as such items by the Employer in a list supplied to the Contractor and annexed to the Employer's Requirements.
Non-Completion Notice:	see **clause 2·28**.
Notice of Completion of Making Good:	see **clause 2·36**.
P&T Rights:	the rights in favour of a Purchaser or Tenant set out in **Part 1 of Schedule 5** or in the appropriate form of collateral warranty.
P&T Rights Particulars:	the entries against **clause 6·12~~11~~** in **Part 1** and the relevant items and entries in that section of **Part 2 of the Contract Particulars**.
Parties:	the Employer and the Contractor together.
Party:	either the Employer or the Contractor.
Pay Less Notice:	see **clauses 4·9·4** and **4·10·2**.
Payment Notice:	see **clauses 4·9·2** and **4·10·1**.
Practical Completion Statement:	see **clause 2·27**.
Pre-agreed Adjustment:	see **clause 2·23·2**.
Principal Contractor:	the Contractor or other contractor named in **Article 6** or any successor appointed by the Employer.
Provisional Sum:	a provisional sum for work included in the Employer's

	Requirements.
Public Holiday:	Christmas Day, Good Friday or a day which under the Banking and Financial Dealings Act 1971 is a bank holiday.[35]
Purchaser:	any person named or otherwise sufficiently identified as such (whether by class or description) in or by the P&T Rights Particulars to whom the Employer transfers or agrees to transfer his interest in all or part of the Works.
Recitals:	the recitals in the **Agreement**.
Rectification Period:	the period stated as such period in the **Contract Particulars** (against the reference to **clause 2·35**) in relation to the Works or (where applicable) a Section.
Relevant Date:	see **clause 2·30**.
Relevant Event:	see **clause 2·26**.
Relevant Matter:	see **clause 4·21**.
Relevant Omission:	see **clause 2·23·3**.
Relevant Part:	see **clause 2·30**.
Retention:	see **clauses** 4·7·2 4·8, and **4·16** to **4·18**.
Retention Percentage:	see **clause 4·18** and the **Contract Particulars**.
Scheme:	Part 1 of the Schedule to The Scheme for Construction Contracts (England and Wales) Regulations 1998.
Sections:	(where applicable) the Sections into which the Works have been divided, as referred to in the **Fifth Recital** and the **Contract Particulars**.
Section Completion Statement:	see **clause 2·27·2**.
Section Sum:	see **clause 2·34** and the **Contract Particulars**.
Site Materials:	all unfixed materials and goods delivered to and placed on or adjacent to the Works which are intended for incorporation therein.
Specified Perils:	see **clause 6·8**.
Statutory Requirements:	any statute, statutory instrument, regulation, rule or order made under any statute or directive having the force of law which affects the Works or performance of any obligations under this Contract and any regulation or bye-law of any local authority or statutory undertaker which has any jurisdiction with regard to the Works or with whose systems the Works are, or are to be, connected, including Development Control Requirements.
Statutory Undertaker:	any local authority or statutory undertaker where executing work solely in pursuance of its statutory obligations, including any persons employed, engaged or authorised by it upon or in connection with that work.
SWMP Regulations:	the Site Waste Management Plans Regulations 2008.
Tenant:	any person named or otherwise sufficiently identified as such (whether by class or description) in or by the P&T Rights Particulars to whom the Employer grants or agrees to grant a

---

[35]   Amend as necessary if different Public Holidays are applicable.

	leasehold interest in all or part of the Works.
Terrorism Cover:	see **clause 6·8**.
Valuation:	a valuation in accordance with the Valuation Rules, pursuant to **clause 5·2**.
Valuation Rules:	see **clauses 5·4** to **5·7**.
VAT:	Value Added Tax.
Works:	the works briefly described in the **First Recital**, as more particularly shown, described or referred to in the Contract Documents, including any changes made to those works in accordance with this Contract.

Interpretation

Reference to clauses etc.

1·2   Unless otherwise stated, a reference in the Agreement or in these Conditions to a clause or Schedule is to that clause in or Schedule to these Conditions and, unless the context otherwise requires, a reference in a Schedule to a paragraph is to that paragraph of that Schedule.

Agreement etc. to be read as a whole

1·3   The Agreement and these Conditions are to be read as a whole but nothing contained in the Employer's Requirements, the Contractor's Proposals or the Contract Sum Analysis, nor anything in any Framework Agreement, shall override or modify the Agreement or these Conditions.

Headings, references to persons, legislation etc.

1·4   In the Agreement and these Conditions, unless the context otherwise requires:

    ·1   the headings are included for convenience only and shall not affect the interpretation of this Contract;

    ·2   the singular includes the plural and vice versa;

    ·3   a gender includes any other gender;

    ·4   a reference to a 'person' includes any individual, firm, partnership, company and any other body corporate; and

    ·5   a reference to a statute, statutory instrument or other subordinate legislation ('legislation') is to such legislation as amended and in force from time to time, including any legislation which re-enacts or consolidates it, with or without modification, and including corresponding legislation in any other relevant part of the United Kingdom.

Reckoning periods of days

1·5   Where under this Contract an act is required to be done within a specified period of days after or from a specified date, the period shall begin immediately after that date. Where the period would include a day which is a Public Holiday that day shall be excluded.

Contracts (Rights of Third Parties) Act 1999

1·6   Other than such rights of any Purchasers, Tenants and/or Funder as take effect pursuant to clauses 7A and/or 7B, nothing in this Contract confers or is intended to confer any right to enforce any of its terms on any person who is not a party to it.

Notices and other communications

1·7   ·1   Any notice or other communication between the Employer (or Employer's Agent) and the Contractor that is expressly referred to in the Agreement or these Conditions (including, without limitation, each application, approval, consent, confirmation, counter-notice, decision, instruction or other notification) shall be in writing.

·2   Subject to clause 1·7·4, each such notice or other communication and any documents to be supplied may or (where so required) shall be sent or transmitted by the means (electronic or otherwise) and in such format as the Parties from time to time agree in writing for the purposes of this Contract.[36]

·3   Subject to clauses 1·7·2 and 1·7·4, any notice, communication or document may be given or served by any effective means and shall be duly given or served if delivered by hand or sent by pre-paid post to:

         ·1   the recipient's address stated in the Contract Particulars, or to such other address as the recipient may from time to time notify to the sender; or

         ·2   if no such address is then current, the recipient's last known principal business address or (where a body corporate) its registered or principal office.

·4   Any notice expressly required by this Contract to be given in accordance with this clause 1·7·4 shall be delivered by hand or sent by Recorded Signed for or Special Delivery post. Where sent by post in that manner, it shall, subject to proof to the contrary, be deemed to have been received on the second Business Day after the date of posting.

·5   If in an emergency any communication is made orally with respect to health and safety, risk of damage to property or insurance matters, written confirmation of it shall be sent as soon thereafter as is reasonably practicable.

Effect of Final Statement

1·8   ·1   As from the due date for the final payment specified in clause 4·12·5 and in addition to the effects referred to in clause 4·12·6, ~~When~~ the Final Statement or, as the case may be, the Employer's Final Statement ('the relevant statement') ~~becomes conclusive as to the balance due between the Parties in accordance with clause 4·12·5, it~~ shall, except as provided in clauses 1·8·2, 1·8·3 and 1·8·4 (and save in respect of fraud), have effect in any proceedings under or arising out of or in connection with this Contract (whether by adjudication, arbitration or legal proceedings) as:

         ·1   conclusive evidence that where and to the extent that any of the particular qualities of any materials or goods or any particular standard of an item of workmanship was described expressly in the Employer's Requirements, or in any instruction issued by the Employer under these Conditions, to be for the approval of the Employer, the particular quality or standard was to the reasonable satisfaction of the Employer, but the relevant statement ~~Final Statement or Employer's Final Statement~~ shall not be conclusive evidence that they or any other materials or goods or workmanship comply with any other requirement or term of this Contract;

         ·2   conclusive evidence that all and only such extensions of time, if any, as are due under clause 2·25 have been given; and

         ·3   conclusive evidence that the reimbursement of direct loss and/or expense, if any, to the Contractor pursuant to clause 4·20 is in final settlement of all and any claims which the Contractor has or may have arising out of the occurrence of any of the Relevant Matters, whether such claim be for breach of contract, duty of care, statutory duty or otherwise.

   ·2   If ~~any~~ adjudication, arbitration or other proceedings have been commenced by either Party before the due date for the final payment ~~the Final Statement or Employer's Final Statement, as the case may be, that~~ the relevant statement shall have effect as provided in clause 1·8·1 upon and from the earlier of either:

         ·1   the conclusion of such proceedings, in which case the statement shall be subject to the terms of any decision, award or judgment in or any settlement of such proceedings; or

         ·2   the expiry of any period of 12 months from or after the submission of the statement, during which neither Party takes any further step in such proceedings, in which case the

---

[36]   The Parties should agree a communications protocol on or before entering into the Contract, or as soon thereafter as is practicable. If the medium or format to be used for the Contractor's Design Submission Procedure (Schedule 1) is not stated in the Employer's Requirements or Contractor's Proposals, that also should be covered by the protocol. See the Design and Build Contract Guide.

statement shall be subject to any terms agreed in settlement of any of the matters previously in issue in such proceedings.

.3 Subject to clause 4·12·6, if If any adjudication, arbitration or other proceedings are commenced by either Party on or after the due date for the final payment and not later than within 28 days after the due date Final Statement or Employer's Final Statement would otherwise become conclusive under clause 4·12·5, the relevant statement shall have effect as conclusive evidence as provided in clause 1·8·1 save only in respect of the matters to which those proceedings relate.

.4 In the case of a dispute or difference on which an Adjudicator gives his decision on a date which is after the due date for the final payment of submission of the Final Statement or Employer's Final Statement, if either Party wishes to have that dispute or difference determined by arbitration or legal proceedings, that Party may commence arbitration or legal proceedings within 28 days of the date on which the Adjudicator gives his decision.

Effect of payments other than payment of Final Statement

1·9 Save as stated in clause 1·8, no payment by the Employer shall of itself be conclusive evidence that any works, any materials or goods or any design to which it relates are in accordance with this Contract.

Applicable law

1·10 This Contract shall be governed by and construed in accordance with the law of England.[37]

---

[37] Where the Parties do not wish the law applicable to this Contract to be the law of England appropriate amendments should be made.

Contractor's Obligations

General obligations

2·1   ·1   The Contractor shall carry out and complete the Works in a proper and workmanlike manner and in compliance with the Contract Documents, the Construction Phase Plan and other Statutory Requirements and for that purpose shall complete the design for the Works including the selection of any specifications for the kinds and standards of the materials, goods and workmanship to be used in the construction of the Works so far as not described or stated in the Employer's Requirements or Contractor's Proposals, and shall give all notices required by the Statutory Requirements.

        ·2   The Contractor's obligation to the Employer to comply with the Statutory Requirements under clause 2·1·1 shall not apply to the extent that the relevant part or parts of the Employer's Requirements state specifically that the Employer's Requirements comply with the Statutory Requirements.

        ·3   The Contractor shall pass to the Employer all approvals received by the Contractor in connection with the Statutory Requirements.

        ·4   The Contractor shall comply with any instruction and be bound by any decision of the Employer issued or made under or pursuant to these Conditions and any such instruction or decision shall have effect except to the extent that it is varied by the Employer or under the dispute resolution procedures of this Contract.

Materials, goods and workmanship

2·2   ·1   All materials and goods for the Works shall, so far as procurable, be of the kinds and standards described in the Employer's Requirements or, if not there specifically described, as described in the Contractor's Proposals or documents referred to in clause 2·8. The Contractor shall not substitute any materials or goods so described without the Employer's consent, which shall not be unreasonably delayed or withheld but shall not relieve the Contractor of his other obligations.

        ·2   Workmanship for the Works shall be of the standards described in the Employer's Requirements or, if not there specifically described, as described in the Contractor's Proposals or documents referred to in clause 2·8.

        ·3   The Contractor shall before carrying out the relevant work and/or ordering the relevant goods or materials provide the Employer with such samples of the standard of workmanship or the quality of the goods or materials which the Contractor intends to provide as are specifically referred to in the Employer's Requirements or in the Contractor's Proposals.

        ·4   The Contractor shall upon the request of the Employer provide him with reasonable proof that the materials and goods used comply with this clause 2·2.

        ·5   The Contractor shall take all reasonable steps to encourage Contractor's Persons to be registered cardholders under the Construction Skills Certification Scheme (CSCS) or qualified under an equivalent recognised qualification scheme.

Possession

Date of Possession – progress

2·3   On the Date of Possession possession of the site or, in the case of a Section, possession of the relevant part of the site shall be given to the Contractor who shall thereupon begin the construction of the Works or Section and regularly and diligently proceed with and complete the same on or before the relevant Completion Date. For the purposes of the Works insurances the Contractor shall retain possession:

    ·1   of the site and the Works up to and including the date of issue of the Practical Completion Statement; or

    ·2   of each Section and the relevant part of the site up to and including the date of issue of the Section Completion Statement for that Section and, in respect of any balance of the site, up to and including the date of issue of the Practical Completion Statement

and, subject to clause 2·30 and section 8, the Employer shall not be entitled to take possession of any part or parts of the Works or Section until such date.

Deferment of possession

2·4   If the Contract Particulars state that clause 2·4 applies in respect of the Works or any Section, the Employer may defer the giving of possession of the site or relevant part of it for a period not exceeding 6 weeks or lesser period stated in the Contract Particulars, calculated from the relevant Date of Possession.

Early use by Employer

2·5   ·1   Notwithstanding clause 2·3, the Employer may, with the Contractor's consent, use or occupy the site or the Works or part of them, whether for storage or otherwise, before the date of issue of the Practical Completion Statement or relevant Section Completion Statement. Before the Contractor gives his consent to such use or occupation, the Contractor or the Employer shall notify the insurers under whichever of Insurance Options A, B or C (paragraph C·2) applies and obtain confirmation that such use or occupation will not prejudice the insurance. Subject to such confirmation, the Contractor's consent shall not be unreasonably delayed or withheld.

    ·2   Where Insurance Option A applies and the insurers' confirmation is conditional on an additional premium being paid, the Contractor shall notify the Employer of the amount of it. If the Employer continues to require such use or occupation, the additional premium shall be added to the Contract Sum and the Contractor shall if requested produce the receipt for it to the Employer.

Work not forming part of the Contract

2·6   In regard to any work not forming part of this Contract which the Employer requires to be carried out by the Employer himself or by any Employer's Persons:

    ·1   where the Employer's Requirements provide the information necessary to enable the Contractor to carry out and complete the Works or each relevant Section in accordance with this Contract, the Contractor shall permit the execution of such work;

    ·2   where the Employer's Requirements do not provide the information referred to in clause 2·6·1, the Employer may with the Contractor's consent arrange for the execution of such work, such consent not to be unreasonably delayed or withheld.

Supply of Documents, Setting Out etc.

Contract Documents

2·7   ·1   The Contract Documents shall remain in the custody of the Employer and shall be available at all reasonable times for inspection by the Contractor.

    ·2   Immediately after the execution of this Contract the Employer, without charge to the Contractor, shall (unless previously provided) provide him with one copy, certified on behalf of the Employer, of the Contract Documents, together with any pre-construction information required for the purposes of regulation 10 of the CDM Regulations.

    ·3   The Contractor shall keep upon the site and available to the Employer's Agent at all reasonable times a copy of each of the following documents, namely: the Employer's Requirements; the Contract Sum Analysis; the Contractor's Proposals; and the drawings and other documents referred to in clause 2·8.

    ·4   Neither Party shall divulge or use except for the purposes of this Contract:

        ·1   the Employer's Requirements, the Contractor's Proposals and the Contract Sum Analysis or any of the documents mentioned in clause 2·8 which the other Party supplies to him; or

   ·2   any confidential information of the other Party,

save that the Employer may use in connection with the maintenance, use, repair, advertisement, letting or sale of the Works any of the documents supplied by the Contractor.

Construction information

2·8   The Contractor shall without charge provide to the Employer copies of the Contractor's Design Documents as and when necessary from time to time in accordance with the Contractor's Design Submission Procedure set out in Schedule 1 or as otherwise stated in the Contract Documents, and the Contractor shall not commence any work to which such a document relates before that procedure has been complied with.

Site boundaries

2·9   The Employer shall define the boundaries of the site.

Discrepancies and Divergences

Divergence in Employer's Requirements and definition of site boundary

2·10 ·1   Any divergence between the Employer's Requirements and the definition of the site boundary as provided under clause 2·9 shall be corrected by an instruction issued by the Employer and such instruction shall be treated as a Change.

     ·2   If the Employer or the Contractor becomes aware of any such divergence he shall immediately give the other notice with details.

Preparation of Employer's Requirements

2·11   Subject to clause 2·15, the Contractor shall not be responsible for the contents of the Employer's Requirements or for verifying the adequacy of any design contained within them.

Employer's Requirements – inadequacy

2·12 ·1   If an inadequacy is found in any design in the Employer's Requirements in relation to which the Contractor under clause 2·11 is not responsible for verifying its adequacy, then, if or to the extent that the inadequacy is not dealt with in the Contractor's Proposals, the Employer's Requirements shall be corrected, altered or modified accordingly.

     ·2   Subject to clause 2·15, any correction, alteration or modification under clause 2·12·1 shall be treated as a Change.

Notice of discrepancies etc.

2·13   If the Contractor becomes aware of any inadequacy as is referred to in clause 2·12 or any other discrepancy or divergence in or between any of the following documents, namely:

     ·1   the Employer's Requirements;

     ·2   the Contractor's Proposals;

     ·3   any instruction issued by the Employer under these Conditions; and

     ·4   any drawings or documents issued under clause 2·8;

he shall immediately give notice with appropriate details to the Employer, who shall issue instructions in that regard.

Discrepancies in documents

2·14 ·1   Where the discrepancy or divergence to be notified under clause 2·13 is within the Contractor's Proposals, the Contractor shall notify the Employer of his proposed amendment to remove it and (subject to compliance with Statutory Requirements) the Employer shall decide between the discrepant items or otherwise may accept the Contractor's proposed amendment; the Contractor shall be obliged to comply with the decision or acceptance by the Employer without cost to the Employer.

·2 Where the discrepancy is within the Employer's Requirements (including any Change to them issued under clause 3·9) the Contractor's Proposals shall prevail (subject to compliance with Statutory Requirements), without any adjustment of the Contract Sum. Where the Contractor's Proposals do not deal with such a discrepancy, the Contractor shall notify the Employer of his proposed amendment to deal with it and the Employer shall either agree the proposed amendment or decide how the discrepancy shall be dealt with; that agreement or decision shall be notified to the Contractor and treated as a Change.

Divergences from Statutory Requirements

2·15 ·1 If the Contractor or Employer becomes aware of any divergence between the Statutory Requirements and

·1 the Employer's Requirements (including any Change); or

·2 the Contractor's Proposals,

he shall immediately give the other notice specifying the divergence and the Contractor shall notify the Employer of his proposed amendment for removing it. With the Employer's consent (which shall not be unreasonably delayed or withheld), the Contractor shall entirely at his own cost, save as provided in clause 2·15·2, complete the design and construction of the Works in accordance with the amendment and the Employer shall note the amendment on the Contract Documents.

·2 ·1 If after the Base Date there is a change in the Statutory Requirements which necessitates an alteration or modification to the Works, such alteration or modification shall be treated as a Change.

·2 If any amendment to the Contractor's Proposals becomes necessary for conformity with the terms of any permission or approval made by a decision of the relevant authority after the Base Date for the purposes of Development Control Requirements, such amendment shall be treated as a Change provided that such treatment is not precluded in the Employer's Requirements.[38]

·3 If any amendment to the part or parts of the Employer's Requirements to which clause 2·1·2 refers becomes necessary for conformity with Statutory Requirements the Employer shall issue an instruction requiring a Change.

Emergency compliance with Statutory Requirements

2·16 ·1 If in any emergency compliance with the Statutory Requirements necessitates the Contractor supplying materials and/or executing work before receiving the Employer's consent under clause 2·15·1, the Contractor shall supply such limited materials and execute such limited work as are reasonably necessary to secure immediate compliance.

·2 The Contractor shall forthwith notify the Employer of the emergency and of the steps that he is taking under clause 2·16·1.

Design Work – liabilities and limitation

2·17 ·1 Insofar as his design of the Works is comprised in the Contractor's Proposals and in what the Contractor is to complete in accordance with the Employer's Requirements and these Conditions (including any further design required to be carried out by the Contractor as a result of a Change), the Contractor shall in respect of any inadequacy in such design have the like liability to the Employer, whether under statute or otherwise, as would an architect or, as the case may be, other appropriate professional designer holding himself out as competent to take on work for such design who, acting independently under a separate contract with the Employer, has supplied such design for or in connection with works to be carried out and completed by a building contractor who is not the supplier of the design.

---

[38] See the Design and Build Contract Guide.

·2   Where and to the extent that this Contract involves the Contractor in taking on work for or in connection with the provision of a dwelling or dwellings, the reference in clause 2·17·1 to the Contractor's liability includes liability under the Defective Premises Act 1972.

·3   Where or to the extent that this Contract does not involve the Contractor in taking on work for or in connection with the provision of a dwelling or dwellings to which the Defective Premises Act 1972 applies, the Contractor's liability for loss of use, loss of profit or other consequential loss arising in respect of the liability of the Contractor referred to in clause 2·17·1 shall be limited to the amount, if any, stated in the Contract Particulars; but such limitation of amount shall not apply to or be affected by any liquidated damages under clause 2·29.

Fees, Royalties and Patent Rights

Fees or charges legally demandable

2·18   The Contractor shall pay all fees or charges (including any rates or taxes) legally demandable under any of the Statutory Requirements and indemnify the Employer against any liability resulting from any failure to do so. No adjustment shall be made to the Contract Sum in respect of the amount of any such fees or charges (including any rates or taxes other than VAT) unless they are stated by way of a Provisional Sum in the Employer's Requirements, in which case clause 4·2 shall apply.

Royalties and patent rights – Contractor's indemnity

2·19   All royalties or other sums payable in respect of the supply and use in carrying out the Works of any patented articles, processes or inventions or in respect of the supply and use for the Works of drawings, or models of buildings that are the subject of copyright, other than drawings or models provided by the Employer, shall be deemed to have been included in the Contract Sum, and the Contractor shall indemnify the Employer from and against all claims and proceedings which may be brought or made against the Employer, and all damages, costs and expense to which he may be put, by reason of the Contractor infringing or being held to have infringed any patent rights in relation to any such articles, processes and inventions or infringing or being held to have infringed copyright.

Patent rights – Instructions

2·20   Where in compliance with the Employer's instructions the Contractor shall supply and/or use in carrying out the Works any patented articles, processes or inventions, the Contractor shall not be liable in respect of any infringement or alleged infringement of any patent rights in relation to any such articles, processes or inventions and all royalties, damages or other sums which the Contractor may be liable to pay to the persons entitled to such rights shall be added to the Contract Sum.

Unfixed Materials and Goods – property, risk etc.

Materials and goods – on site

2·21   Site Materials shall not be removed from storage on or adjacent to the Works except for use on the Works without the Employer's consent, such consent not to be unreasonably delayed or withheld. Where their value has been included in any Interim Payment, they shall upon such payment become the Employer's property, but, subject to Insurance Option B or C (if applicable), the Contractor shall remain responsible for loss or damage to them.

Materials and goods – off site

2·22   Where the value of any Listed Items has in accordance with clause 4·15 been included in any Interim Payment, those items shall become the Employer's property and thereafter the Contractor shall not, except for use upon the Works, remove or cause or permit them to be moved or removed from the premises where they are. The Contractor shall be responsible for any loss of or damage to them and for the cost of their storage, handling and insurance until they are delivered to and placed on or adjacent to the Works. As from such delivery the provisions of clause 2·21 (except the words "Where their value" to "Employer's property, but,") shall apply to such items.

Adjustment of Completion Date

Related definitions and interpretation

2·23   In clauses 2·24 to 2·26 and, so far as relevant, in the other clauses of these Conditions:

.1 any reference to delay or extension of time includes any further delay or further extension of time;

.2 'Pre-agreed Adjustment' means the fixing of a revised Completion Date for the Works or a Section under paragraph 4 of the Supplemental Provisions or by the Confirmed Acceptance of an Acceleration Quotation;

.3 'Relevant Omission' means the omission of any work or obligation through an instruction for a Change under clause 3·9.

Notice by Contractor of delay to progress

2·24 .1 If and whenever it becomes reasonably apparent that the progress of the Works or any Section is being or is likely to be delayed the Contractor shall forthwith give notice to the Employer of the material circumstances, including the cause or causes of the delay, and shall identify in the notice any event which in his opinion is a Relevant Event.

.2 In respect of each event identified in the notice the Contractor shall, if practicable in such notice or otherwise in writing as soon as possible thereafter, give particulars of its expected effects, including an estimate of any expected delay in the completion of the Works or any Section beyond the relevant Completion Date.

.3 The Contractor shall forthwith notify the Employer of any material change in the estimated delay or in any other particulars and supply such further information as the Employer may at any time reasonably require.

Fixing Completion Date

2·25 .1 If on receiving a notice and particulars under clause 2·24:

.1 any of the events which are stated to be a cause of delay is a Relevant Event; and

.2 completion of the Works or of any Section is likely to be delayed thereby beyond the relevant Completion Date,

then, save where these Conditions expressly provide otherwise, the Employer shall give an extension of time by fixing such later date as the Completion Date for the Works or Section as he then estimates to be fair and reasonable.

.2 Whether or not an extension is given, the Employer shall notify the Contractor of his decision in respect of any notice under clause 2·24 as soon as is reasonably practicable and in any event within 12 weeks of receipt of the required particulars. Where the period from receipt to the Completion Date is less than 12 weeks, he shall endeavour to do so prior to the Completion Date.

.3 The Employer shall in his decision state:

.1 the extension of time that he has attributed to each Relevant Event; and

.2 (in the case of a decision under clause 2·25·4 or 2·25·5) the reduction in time that he has attributed to each Relevant Omission.

.4 After the first fixing of a later Completion Date in respect of the Works or a Section, either under clause 2·25·1 or by a Pre-agreed Adjustment, but subject to clauses 2·25·6·3 and 2·25·6·4, the Employer may by notice to the Contractor, giving the details referred to in clause 2·25·3, fix a Completion Date for the Works or that Section earlier than that previously so fixed if the fixing of such earlier Completion Date is fair and reasonable, having regard to any Relevant Omissions for which instructions have been issued after the last occasion on which a new Completion Date was fixed for the Works or for that Section.

.5 After the Completion Date for the Works or for a Section, if this occurs before the date of practical completion, the Employer may, and not later than the expiry of 12 weeks after the date of practical completion shall, by notice to the Contractor, giving the details referred to in clause 2·25·3:

　　　　　　　·1　　fix a Completion Date for the Works or for the Section later than that previously fixed if it is fair and reasonable having regard to any Relevant Events, whether on reviewing a previous decision or otherwise and whether or not the Relevant Event has been specifically notified by the Contractor under clause 2·24·1; or

　　　　　　　·2　　subject to clauses 2·25·6·3 and 2·25·6·4, fix a Completion Date earlier than that previously fixed if that is fair and reasonable having regard to any instructions for Relevant Omissions issued after the last occasion on which a new Completion Date was fixed for the Works or Section; or

　　　　　　　·3　　confirm the Completion Date previously fixed.

　　　·6　　Provided always that:

　　　　　　　·1　　the Contractor shall constantly use his best endeavours to prevent delay in the progress of the Works or any Section, however caused, and to prevent the completion of the Works or Section being delayed or further delayed beyond the relevant Completion Date;

　　　　　　　·2　　in the event of any delay the Contractor shall do all that may reasonably be required to the satisfaction of the Employer to proceed with the Works or Section;

　　　　　　　·3　　no decision of the Employer under clause 2·25·4 or 2·25·5·2 shall fix a Completion Date for the Works or any Section earlier than the relevant Date for Completion; and

　　　　　　　·4　　no decision under clause 2·25·4 or 2·25·5·2 shall alter the length of any Pre-agreed Adjustment except where that adjustment relates to a Change and that Change is itself the subject of a Relevant Omission.

Relevant Events

2·26　　The following are the Relevant Events referred to in clauses 2·24 and 2·25:

　　　·1　　Changes and any other matters or instructions which under these Conditions are to be treated as, or as requiring, a Change;

　　　·2　　Employer's instructions:

　　　　　　　·1　　under clause 2·13, except for any instructions relating to a discrepancy or divergence in or between the Contractor's Proposals and/or any drawings or documents issued under clause 2·8;

　　　　　　　·2　　under ~~any of~~ clauses 3·10~~,~~ or 3·11 ~~or 3·15·2~~; or

　　　　　　　·3　　for the opening up for inspection or testing of any work, materials or goods under clause 3·12 or 3·13·3 (including making good), unless the inspection or test shows that the work, materials or goods are not in accordance with this Contract;

　　　·3　　deferment of the giving of possession of the site or any Section under clause 2·4;

　　　·4　　compliance with clause 3·15·1 or with the Employer's instructions under clause 3·15·2;

　　　·5̶4̶　　suspension by the Contractor under clause 4·11 of the performance of any or all of his obligations under this Contract;

　　　·6̶5̶　　any impediment, prevention or default, whether by act or omission, by the Employer or any of the Employer's Persons, except to the extent caused or contributed to by any default, whether by act or omission, of the Contractor or of any of the Contractor's Persons;

　　　·7̶6̶　　the carrying out by a Statutory Undertaker of work in pursuance of its statutory obligations in relation to the Works, or the failure to carry out such work;

　　　·8̶7̶　　exceptionally adverse weather conditions;

　　　·9̶8̶　　loss or damage occasioned by any of the Specified Perils;

　　　·10̶9̶　　civil commotion or the use or threat of terrorism and/or the activities of the relevant authorities in dealing with such event or threat;

·11+
0 strike, lock-out or local combination of workmen affecting any of the trades employed upon the Works or any of the trades engaged in the preparation, manufacture or transportation of any of the goods or materials required for the Works or any persons engaged in the preparation of the design for the Works;

·12+
1 the exercise after the Base Date by the United Kingdom Government of any statutory power which directly affects the execution of the Works;

·13+
2 delay in receipt of any necessary permission or approval of any statutory body which the Contractor has taken all practicable steps to avoid or reduce;

·14+
3 force majeure.

Practical Completion, Lateness and Liquidated Damages

Practical completion

2·27 When practical completion of the Works or a Section is achieved and the Contractor has complied sufficiently with clauses 2·37 and 3·16·5, then:

·1 in the case of the Works, the Employer shall forthwith issue a statement to that effect ('the Practical Completion Statement');

·2 in the case of a Section, he shall forthwith issue a statement of practical completion of that Section (a 'Section Completion Statement');

and practical completion of the Works or the Section shall be deemed for all the purposes of this Contract to have taken place on the date stated in that statement.

Non-Completion Notice

2·28 If the Contractor fails to complete the Works or a Section by the relevant Completion Date, the Employer shall issue a notice to that effect (a 'Non-Completion Notice'). If a new Completion Date is fixed after the issue of such a notice, such fixing shall cancel that notice and the Employer shall where necessary issue a further notice.

Payment or allowance of liquidated damages

2·29 ·1 Provided:

·1 the Employer has issued a Non-Completion Notice for the Works or a Section; and

·2 the Employer has notified the Contractor before the due date for the final payment under clause 4·12·5 date when the Final Statement (or, as the case may be, the Employer's Final Statement) becomes conclusive as to the balance due between the Parties that he may require payment of, or may withhold or deduct, liquidated damages,

the Employer may, not later than 5 days before the final date for payment of the amount payable debt due under clause 4·12, give notice to the Contractor in the terms set out in clause 2·29·2.

·2 A notice from the Employer under clause 2·29·1 shall state that for the period between the Completion Date and the date of practical completion of the Works or that Section:

·1 he requires the Contractor to pay liquidated damages at the rate stated in the Contract Particulars, or lesser rate stated in the notice, in which event the Employer may recover the same as a debt; and/or

·2 that he will withhold or deduct liquidated damages at the rate stated in the Contract Particulars, or at such lesser stated rate, from sums due to the Contractor.[39]

---

[39] In addition to the notice under clause 2·29·2, the Employer, if he intends to withhold or deduct all or any of the liquidated damages payable, must give the appropriate Pay Less Notice under clause 4·9·4 or 4·12·8. Where the Employer intends to withhold all or any of the liquidated damages payable, either the notice under clause 2·29·2 must comply with the requirements of clause 4·10·4 or 4·12·9 or a separate notice that complies with those requirements must be given.

·3   If the Employer fixes a later Completion Date for the Works or a Section, the Employer shall pay or repay to the Contractor any amounts recovered, allowed or paid under clause 2·29 for the period up to that later Completion Date.

·4   If the Employer in relation to the Works or a Section has notified the Contractor in accordance with clause 2·29·1·2 that he may require payment of, or may withhold or deduct, liquidated damages, then, unless the Employer states otherwise in writing, clause 2·29·1·2 shall remain satisfied in relation to the Works or Section, notwithstanding the cancellation of the relevant Non-Completion Notice and issue of any further Non-Completion Notice.

Partial Possession by Employer

Contractor's consent

2·30   If at any time or times before the Practical Completion Statement or relevant Section Completion Statement the Employer wishes to take possession of any part or parts of the Works or a Section and the Contractor's consent has been obtained (which consent shall not be unreasonably delayed or withheld), then, notwithstanding anything expressed or implied elsewhere in this Contract, the Employer may take possession of such part or parts. The Contractor shall thereupon give the Employer notice identifying the part or parts taken into possession and giving the date when the Employer took possession ('the Relevant Part' and 'the Relevant Date' respectively).

Practical completion date

2·31   For the purposes of clauses 2·35 and 4·18·2, practical completion of the Relevant Part shall be deemed to have occurred, and the Rectification Period in respect of the Relevant Part shall be deemed to have commenced, on the Relevant Date.

Defects etc. – Relevant Part

2·32   When any defects, shrinkages or other faults in the Relevant Part which the Employer has required to be made good under clause 2·35 have been made good, he shall issue a notice to that effect.

Insurance – Relevant Part

2·33   As from the Relevant Date the insurance obligation of the Contractor under Insurance Option A or of the Employer under Insurance Option B or paragraph C·2 of Insurance Option C (whichever applies) shall terminate in respect of the Relevant Part (but not otherwise); and, where Insurance Option C applies, the obligation of the Employer to insure under paragraph C·1 shall from the Relevant Date include the Relevant Part.

Liquidated damages – Relevant Part

2·34   As from the Relevant Date, the rate of liquidated damages stated in the Contract Particulars in respect of the Works or Section containing the Relevant Part shall reduce by the same proportion as the value of the Relevant Part bears to the Contract Sum or to the relevant Section Sum, as shown in the Contract Particulars.

Defects

Schedules of defects and instructions

2·35   If any defects, shrinkages or other faults in the Works or a Section appear within the relevant Rectification Period due to any failure of the Contractor to comply with his obligations under this Contract:

·1   such defects, shrinkages and other faults shall be specified by the Employer in a schedule of defects which he shall deliver to the Contractor as an instruction not later than 14 days after the expiry of that Rectification Period; and

·2   notwithstanding clause 2·35·1, the Employer may whenever he considers it necessary issue instructions requiring any such defect, shrinkage or other fault to be made good, provided no instructions under this clause 2·35·2 shall be issued after delivery of a schedule of defects or more than 14 days after the expiry of the relevant Rectification Period.

Within a reasonable time after receipt of such schedule or instructions, the defects, shrinkages and other faults shall at no cost to the Employer be made good by the Contractor unless the Employer shall otherwise instruct. If he does so otherwise instruct, an appropriate deduction shall be made from the Contract Sum in respect of the defects, shrinkages or other faults not made good.

Notice of Completion of Making Good

2·36 When the defects, shrinkages or other faults in the Works or a Section which the Employer has required to be made good under clause 2·35 have been made good, he shall issue a notice to that effect (a 'Notice of Completion of Making Good'). That notice shall not be unreasonably delayed or withheld, and completion of that making good shall for the purposes of this Contract be deemed to have taken place on the date stated in that notice.

Contractor's Design Documents

As-built Drawings

2·37 The Contractor, before practical completion of the Works or relevant Section, shall without further charge to the Employer supply for the retention and use of the Employer such Contractor's Design Documents and related information as may be specified in the Contract Documents or as the Employer may reasonably require, showing or describing the Works as built and, without affecting the Contractor's obligations under clause 3·16 (*the health and safety file*), concerning the maintenance and operation of the Works, including any installations forming part of it.

Copyright and use

2·38 ·1 Subject to any rights in any designs, drawings and other documents supplied to the Contractor for the purposes of this Contract by or on behalf of the Employer, the copyright in all Contractor's Design Documents shall remain vested in the Contractor.

·2 Subject to all sums due and payable under this Contract to the Contractor having been paid, the Employer shall have an irrevocable, royalty-free, non-exclusive licence to copy and use the Contractor's Design Documents and to reproduce the designs and content of them for any purpose relating to the Works including, without limitation, the construction, completion, maintenance, letting, sale, promotion, advertisement, reinstatement, refurbishment and repair of the Works. Such licence shall enable the Employer to copy and use the Contractor's Design Documents for the extension of the Works but shall not include a licence to reproduce the designs contained in them for any extension of the Works.

·3 The Contractor shall not be liable for any use by the Employer of any of the Contractor's Design Documents for any purpose other than that for which they were prepared.

Access and Representatives

Access for Employer's Agent

3·1   The Employer's Agent and any person authorised by him or the Employer shall at all reasonable times have access to the Works and to the workshops or other premises of the Contractor where work is being prepared for this Contract. When work is to be prepared in workshops or other premises of a sub-contractor the Contractor shall by a term in the sub-contract secure so far as possible a similar right of access to those workshops or premises for the Employer and any person authorised by him and shall do all things reasonably necessary to make that right effective. Access under this clause 3·1 may be subject to such reasonable restrictions as are necessary to protect proprietary rights.

Person-in-charge

3·2   The Contractor shall ensure that at all times he has on the site a competent person-in-charge and any instructions given to that person by the Employer shall be deemed to have been issued to the Contractor.

Sub-Contracting

Consent to sub-contracting

3·3   ·1   The Contractor shall not without the Employer's consent sub-contract the whole or any part of the Works. Such consent shall not be unreasonably delayed or withheld but the Contractor shall remain wholly responsible for carrying out and completing the Works in all respects in accordance with clause 2·1 notwithstanding any such sub-contracting.

     ·2   The Contractor shall not without the Employer's consent sub-contract the design for the Works. Such consent shall not be unreasonably delayed or withheld but shall not in any way affect the obligations of the Contractor under clause 2·17 or any other provision of this Contract.

     ·3   The provisions of this clause 3·3 and of clause 3·4 shall not apply to the execution of part of the Works by a Statutory Undertaker, who shall not in that capacity be a sub-contractor within the terms of this Contract.

Conditions of sub-contracting

3·4   Where considered appropriate, the Contractor shall engage the Sub-Contractor using the JCT Design and Build Sub-Contract. It shall be a condition of any sub-contract that[40]:

     ·1   the employment of the sub-contractor under the sub-contract shall terminate immediately upon the termination (for any reason) of the Contractor's employment under this Contract;

     ·2   the sub-contract shall provide:

         ·1   that, except for use on the Works, no Site Materials delivered to the Works by or for the sub-contractor shall be removed without the Contractor's written consent (such consent not to be unreasonably delayed or withheld) and that:

             ·1   where, in accordance with clauses 4·7·2 4·8 and 4·13 or 4·14 of these Conditions, the value of any Site Materials has been included in any Interim Payment and that Interim Payment has been paid by the Employer to the Contractor, they shall

---

[40]   The requirements of clauses 3·4·1 and 3·4·2 together with those in paragraphs A·3 and B·4 of the Fluctuations Options (Schedule 7) are met by the JCT Design and Build Sub-Contract (DBSub).

upon such payment become the Employer's property and the sub-contractor shall not deny that they have become the Employer's property;

    ·2   if the Contractor pays the sub-contractor for any Site Materials before their value is included in any Interim Payment, they shall upon such payment become the Contractor's property;

·2   for the grant by the sub-contractor of the rights of access to workshops or other premises referred to in clause 3·1 of these Conditions;

·3   that each party undertakes to the other in relation to the Works and the site duly to comply with the CDM Regulations;

·4   that if by the final date for payment stated in the sub-contract the Contractor fails ~~properly~~ to pay a sum ~~any amount~~, or any part of it, due to the sub-contractor, the Contractor shall, in addition to any unpaid amount that should properly have been paid, ~~the amount not properly paid~~ pay simple interest on that amount at the Interest Rate for the period from the final date for payment until such payment is made; such payment of interest to be on and subject to terms equivalent to those of clauses 4·9·5 ~~4·10·6~~ and 4·12·10 ~~4·12·9~~ of these Conditions;

·5   where applicable, for the execution and delivery by the sub-contractor, in each case within 14 days of receipt of a written request by the Contractor, of such collateral warranties as comply with the Contract Documents;

·6   that neither of the provisions referred to in clauses 3·4·2·1·1 and 3·4·2·1·2 shall operate so as to affect any vesting in the Contractor of property in any Listed Item required for the purposes of clause 4·15·2·1 of these Conditions.

The Contractor shall not give such consent as is referred to in clause 3·4·2·1 without the prior consent of the Employer under clause 2·21 of these Conditions.

Employer's Instructions

Compliance with instructions

3·5   The Contractor shall forthwith comply with all instructions issued to him by the Employer in regard to any matter in respect of which the Employer is expressly empowered by these Conditions to issue instructions, save that where an instruction requires a Change of the type referred to in clause 5·1·2 the Contractor need not comply to the extent that he notifies a reasonable objection to it to the Employer.

Non-compliance with instructions

3·6   Subject to clauses 3·5 and 3·9, if within 7 days after receipt of a notice from the Employer requiring compliance with an instruction the Contractor does not comply, the Employer may employ and pay other persons to execute any work whatsoever which may be necessary to give effect to that instruction. The Contractor shall be liable for all additional costs incurred by the Employer in connection with such employment and an appropriate deduction shall be made from the Contract Sum.

Instructions other than in writing

3·7 ·1   Where the Employer issues an instruction otherwise than in writing, it shall be of no immediate effect but the Contractor shall confirm it in writing to the Employer within 7 days, and, if he does not dissent by notice to the Contractor within 7 days from receipt of the Contractor's confirmation, it shall take effect as from the expiry of the latter 7 day period.

    ·2   If within 7 days of giving an instruction otherwise than in writing the Employer confirms it in writing, the Contractor shall not be obliged to confirm it and it shall take effect as from the date of the Employer's confirmation.

    ·3   If neither the Contractor nor the Employer confirms such an instruction in the manner and time stated but the Contractor nevertheless complies with it, the Employer may at any time prior to the due date for the final payment under clause 4·12·5 ~~Final Statement or Employer's Final Statement becoming conclusive as to the balance due between the Parties~~ confirm it with retrospective effect.

Provisions empowering instructions

3·8 On receipt of an instruction or purported instruction the Contractor may request the Employer to notify him which provision of these Conditions empowers its issue and the Employer shall forthwith comply with the request. If the Contractor thereafter complies with that instruction with neither Party then having invoked any dispute resolution procedure under this Contract to establish the Employer's powers in that regard, the instruction shall be deemed to have been duly given under the specified provision.

Instructions requiring Changes

3·9 ·1 The Employer may issue instructions requiring a Change, subject to clause 3·9·4 and provided that the Employer may not effect a Change which is, or which makes necessary, an alteration or modification in the design of the Works without the Contractor's consent, which consent shall not be unreasonably delayed or withheld.

·2 Any instruction of the type referred to in clause 5·1·2 shall be subject to the Contractor's right of reasonable objection set out in clause 3·5.

·3 No Change required by the Employer or subsequently sanctioned by him shall vitiate this Contract.

·4 The Contractor shall, within a reasonable time after receipt of an instruction effecting a Change or of an instruction in regard to the expenditure of a Provisional Sum included in the Employer's Requirements, notify the Employer whether, pursuant to his obligations under regulation 20 (if he is the CDM Co-ordinator) or regulation 22 of the CDM Regulations, he has any objection to such instruction. If the Contractor has any reasonable objection the Employer shall, to the reasonable satisfaction of the Contractor, vary the terms of the instruction so as to remove that objection; and, until the Employer has so varied the terms of the instruction, the Contractor shall not be required pursuant to clause 2·1 to comply with such instruction.

Postponement of work

3·10 The Employer may issue instructions in regard to the postponement of any work to be executed under this Contract.

Instructions on Provisional Sums

3·11 The Employer shall issue instructions in regard to the expenditure of Provisional Sums included in the Employer's Requirements.

Inspection – tests

3·12 The Employer may issue instructions requiring the Contractor to open up for inspection any work covered up or to arrange for or carry out any test of any materials or goods (whether or not already incorporated in the Works) or of any executed work. The cost of such opening up or testing (including the cost of making good) shall be added to the Contract Sum unless provided for in the Employer's Requirements or in the Contractor's Proposals or unless the inspection or test shows that the materials, goods or work are not in accordance with this Contract.

Work not in accordance with the Contract

3·13 If any work, materials or goods are not in accordance with this Contract the Employer, in addition to his other powers, may:

·1 issue instructions in regard to the removal from the site of all or any of such work, materials or goods;

·2 after consultation with the Contractor, issue such instructions requiring a Change (to which the proviso in clause 3·9·1 applies) as are reasonably necessary as a consequence of any instruction under clause 3·13·1 (but to the extent that such instructions are reasonably necessary, no addition shall be made to the Contract Sum and no extension of time shall be given); and/or

·3 having due regard to the Code of Practice set out in Schedule 4, issue such instructions under clause 3·12 to open up for inspection or to test as are reasonable in all the circumstances to establish to the reasonable satisfaction of the Employer the likelihood or extent, as appropriate to the circumstances, of any further similar non-compliance. To the extent that such instructions are reasonable, whatever the results of the opening up, no addition shall be made to the Contract Sum but clauses 2·25 and 2·26·2·32 shall apply unless the inspection or test shows that the work, materials or goods are not in accordance with this Contract.

Workmanship not in accordance with the Contract

3·14   Where there is any failure to comply with clause 2·1 in regard to the carrying out of work in a proper and workmanlike manner and/or in accordance with the Construction Phase Plan, the Employer, in addition to his other powers, may, after consultation with the Contractor, issue such instructions (whether requiring a Change or otherwise) as are in consequence reasonably necessary. To the extent that such instructions are reasonably necessary, no addition shall be made to the Contract Sum and no extension of time shall be given.

Antiquities

3·15   ·1   All fossils, antiquities and other objects of interest or value which may be found on the site or in excavating it during the progress of the Works shall become the Employer's property. Upon discovery of any such object the Contractor shall forthwith:

·1   use his best endeavours not to disturb the object and cease work if and insofar as its continuance would endanger the object or prevent or impede its excavation or removal;

·2   take all steps necessary to preserve the object in the exact position and condition in which it was found; and

·3   inform the Employer of its discovery and precise location.

·2   The Employer shall issue instructions as to action to be taken concerning any object reported under clause 3·15·1, which (without limiting his powers) may require the Contractor to permit the examination, excavation or removal of the object by a third party.

CDM Regulations

Undertakings to comply

3·16   Each Party acknowledges that he is aware of and undertakes to the other that in relation to the Works and site he will duly comply with the CDM Regulations. Without limitation, where the project that comprises or includes the Works is notifiable:

·1   where the Contractor is not the CDM Co-ordinator, the Employer shall ensure that the CDM Co-ordinator carries out all his duties and, where the Contractor is not the Principal Contractor, shall ensure that the Principal Contractor carries out all his duties under those regulations;

·2   where the Contractor is and while he remains the CDM Co-ordinator, he shall comply with all the duties of a CDM Co-ordinator and shall without charge prepare, and deliver to the Employer, the health and safety file;

·3   where the Contractor is and while he remains the Principal Contractor, he shall ensure that:

·1   the Construction Phase Plan is prepared and received by the Employer before construction work under this Contract is commenced, and that any subsequent amendment to it by the Contractor is notified to the Employer and the CDM Co-ordinator; and

·2   welfare facilities complying with Schedule 2 of the CDM Regulations are provided from the commencement of construction work until the end of the construction phase[41];

·4   where the Contractor is not the Principal Contractor, he shall promptly notify the Principal Contractor of the identity of each sub-contractor that he appoints and each sub-subcontractor appointment notified to him;

---

[41]   There is a duty on contractors to ensure compliance with Schedule 2 of the CDM Regulations so far as is reasonably practicable, whether or not the project is notifiable and whether or not the contractor is the Principal Contractor.

.5   where the Contractor is not or ceases to be the CDM Co-ordinator, the Contractor shall promptly upon the written request of the CDM Co-ordinator provide, and shall ensure that any sub-contractor, through the Contractor, provides, to the CDM Co-ordinator (or, if the Contractor is not the Principal Contractor, to the Principal Contractor) such information as the CDM Co-ordinator reasonably requires for the preparation of the health and safety file.

Appointment of successors

3·17   If the Employer by a further appointment replaces the CDM Co-ordinator or the Principal Contractor, the Employer shall immediately upon such further appointment notify the Contractor of the name and address of the new appointee. If the Employer appoints a successor to the Contractor as the Principal Contractor, the Contractor shall at no cost to the Employer comply with all reasonable requirements of the new Principal Contractor to the extent necessary for compliance with the CDM Regulations; no extension of time shall be given in respect of such compliance.

Contract Sum and Adjustments

Adjustment only under the Conditions

4·1   The Contract Sum shall not be adjusted or altered in any way other than in accordance with the express provisions of these Conditions.

Items included in adjustments

4·2   ·1   The Contract Sum shall be adjusted by:

         ·1   any amounts agreed by the Employer and the Contractor in respect of Changes or other work of the types referred to in clause 5·2;

         ·2   the amount stated in any Acceleration Quotation for which there is a Confirmed Acceptance; and

         ·3   (where Insurance Option A applies) any variation in premium referred to in clause 6·10·2 paragraph A·5·1 of Schedule 3.

   ·2   There shall be deducted from the Contract Sum:

         ·1   all Provisional Sums included in the Employer's Requirements;

         ·2   the amount of each Valuation under clause 5·4·3 of items omitted in accordance with a Change, together with the amount included in the Contract Sum Analysis for any other work as referred to in clause 5·6;

         ·3   any amounts deductible under clause 2·10·1, 2·15·2, 2·35, 3·6, 6·5·3 or 6·16 15·2 and any amounts allowable to the Employer under whichever Fluctuations Option applies; and

         ·4   any other amount required by this Contract to be deducted from the Contract Sum.

   ·3   There shall be added to the Contract Sum:

         ·1   any amounts payable by the Employer to the Contractor as a result of payments made or costs incurred by the Contractor under clauses 2·10·1, 2·15·2, 2·20 and 3·12;

         ·2   the amount of the Valuation of any Change, including the Valuation of other work as referred to in clause 5·6 but excluding any omission;

         ·3   the amount of each Valuation of work executed by, or the amount of any disbursements by, the Contractor in accordance with Employer's instructions as to the expenditure of Provisional Sums included in the Employer's Requirements;

         ·4   any amounts ascertained under clause 4·20;

         ·5   any amounts paid by the Contractor under Insurance Option B or C or under clause 2·5·2, 6·10·3, 6·11·3 or 6·17 which the Contractor is entitled to have added to the Contract Sum;

         ·6   any amounts payable to the Contractor under whichever Fluctuations Option applies; and

         ·7   any amounts payable under clause 4·11·2; and

         ·8 7   any other amount required by this Contract to be added to the Contract Sum.

Taking adjustments into account

4·3   Where these Conditions provide that an amount is to be added to, deducted from or dealt with by adjustment of the Contract Sum, then, as soon as the amount is ascertained in whole or in part, the ascertained amount shall be taken into account in the next Interim Payment.

Payments and Notices

VAT

4·4   ·1   The Contract Sum is exclusive of VAT and in relation to any payment to the Contractor under this Contract, the Employer shall in addition pay the amount of any VAT properly chargeable in respect of it.

        ·2   To the extent that after the Base Date the supply of goods and services to the Employer becomes exempt from VAT there shall be paid to the Contractor an amount equal to the amount of input tax on the supply to the Contractor of goods and services which contribute to the Works but which as a consequence of that exemption the Contractor cannot recover.

Construction Industry Scheme (CIS)

4·5   If the Employer is or at any time up to the final payment ~~of the balance~~ under clause 4·12~~·10~~ becomes a 'contractor' for the purposes of the CIS[42], his obligation to make any payment under this Contract is subject to the provisions of the CIS.

Advance payment

4·6   Where the Contract Particulars state that clause 4·6 applies, the advance payment shall be paid to the Contractor on the date and reimbursed to the Employer on the terms stated in the Contract Particulars. Provided that where the Contract Particulars state that an advance payment bond is required, payment shall only be made if the Contractor has provided to the Employer a bond in the terms set out in Part 1 of Schedule 6 from a surety approved by the Employer.[43]

Issue and amount of Interim Payments

4·7   ·1   Interim Payments shall be made by the Employer to the Contractor in accordance with section 4 and whichever of Alternatives A (Stage Payments~~clause 4·13~~) or Alternative B (Periodic Payments~~clause 4·14~~) is stated in the Contract Particulars to apply.

~~Amounts due in Interim Payments~~

4·8   ·2   The ~~amount~~ sum due as an Interim Payment shall be an amount equal to the Gross Valuation ~~pursuant to~~ under clause 4·13 where Alternative A applies, or clause 4·14 where Alternative B applies, ~~whichever is applicable,~~ in either case less the aggregate of:

        ~~·1~~   ·1   any amount which may be deducted and retained by the Employer as provided in clauses 4·16 and 4·18 ('the Retention');

        ~~·2~~   ·2   the cumulative total of the amounts of any advance payment that have then become due for reimbursement to the Employer in accordance with the terms stated in the Contract Particulars for clause 4·6; and

        ~~·3~~   ·3   the amounts paid in previous Interim Payments.

Contractor's Interim Applications and due dates ~~by Contractor~~

4·9   ~~The Contractor shall make Applications for Interim Payment as follows:~~

4·8   ·1   In relation to each Interim Payment, the Contractor shall make an application to the Employer (an 'Interim Application') in accordance with the following provisions of this clause 4·8, stating the sum that the Contractor considers to be due to him and the basis on which that sum has been calculated.

---

[42]   See the Contract Particulars (Fourth Recital and clause 4·5).

[43]   As to approval of sureties, see the Design and Build Contract Guide.

·2~~1~~ ~~w~~Where Alternative A applies, an ~~Application for~~ Interim Application ~~Payment~~ shall be made as at ~~on~~ completion of each stage specified in or by ~~set out in~~ the Contract Particulars for Alternative A. ~~and, from~~ Following the application in respect of the last stage, such applications shall be made at intervals of 2 months (unless otherwise agreed), the last such application being made ~~and~~ upon ~~whichever is the later of~~ the expiry of the Rectification Period or, if later, the issue of the Notice of Completion of Making Good (or, where there are Sections, the last such period or notice)~~;~~. The due date for payment (the 'due date') in each case shall be the later of the date of completion of the stage (or, when applicable, the 2 monthly date) and the date of receipt by the Employer of the Interim Application.

·3~~2~~ ~~w~~Where Alternative B applies, for the period up to practical completion of the Works, Interim Applications ~~for Interim Payment~~ shall be made as at ~~on~~ the monthly dates ~~provided for~~ specified in the Contract Particulars for Alternative B up to the date of practical completion ~~named in the Employer's Practical Completion Statement~~ or the specified date within one month thereafter. Subsequent Interim Applications ~~for Interim Payment~~ shall ~~thereafter~~ be made at intervals of 2 months (unless otherwise agreed), the last such application being made ~~and~~ upon ~~whichever is the later of~~ the expiry of the Rectification Period or, if later, the issue of the Notice of Completion of Making Good (or, where there are Sections, the last such period or notice)~~;~~. The due date in each case shall be the later of the specified date and the date of receipt by the Employer of the Interim Application.

·4~~3~~ ~~each Application for~~ Interim Applications may be made before, on or after completion of the relevant stage or the monthly date and ~~Payment~~ shall be accompanied by such further information ~~details~~ as may be specified ~~stated~~ in the Employer's Requirements.

Interim Payments – final date and amount

4·9~~10~~ ·1 The final date for payment of an Interim Payment shall be 14 days from its due date ~~the date of receipt by the Employer of the Application for Interim Payment~~.

·2 ~~Notwithstanding his fiduciary interest in the Retention as stated in clause 4·16, the Employer is entitled to exercise any rights under this Contract of withholding or deduction from sums due or to become due to the Contractor against any amount otherwise due, whether or not any Retention is included in that amount under clause 4·18.~~

·2~~3~~ Not later than 5 days after the due date ~~receipt of an Application for Interim Payment~~ the Employer shall give a notice (a 'Payment Notice') to the Contractor in accordance with clause 4·10·1 and, subject to any Pay Less Notice given by the Employer under clause 4·9·4, the amount of the Interim Payment to be made by the Employer on or before the final date for payment shall be the sum stated as due in the Payment Notice. ~~which shall, in respect of that application, specify the amount of the payment proposed to be made, to what the amount relates and the basis on which the amount has been calculated.~~

·3 If the Payment Notice is not given in accordance with clause 4·9·2, the amount of the Interim Payment to be made by the Employer shall, subject to any Pay Less Notice under clause 4·9·4, be the sum stated as due in the Interim Application.

·4 If the Employer intends to pay less than the sum stated as due from him in the Payment Notice or Interim Application, as the case may be, he shall not later than 5 days before the final date for payment give the Contractor notice of that intention in accordance with clause 4·10·2 (a 'Pay Less Notice'). Where a Pay Less Notice is given, the payment to be made on or before the final date for payment shall not be less than the amount stated as due in the notice.

·4 ~~Not later than 5 days before the final date for payment the Employer may give a notice to the Contractor which shall specify any amount proposed to be withheld or deducted from the amount due, the ground or grounds for such withholding or deduction and the amount of withholding or deduction attributable to each ground.~~

·5 ~~Subject to any notice given under clause 4·10·4, the Employer shall no later than the final date for payment pay the Contractor the amount specified in the notice given under clause 4·10·3 or, in the absence of a notice under clause 4·10·3, the amount due to the Contractor as determined in accordance with clause 4·8.~~

·5~~6~~ If the Employer fails ~~properly~~ to pay a sum ~~the amount~~, or any part of it, due to the Contractor under these Conditions by the final date for its payment, the Employer shall, in addition to any unpaid amount that should properly have been paid ~~the amount not properly paid~~, pay the Contractor simple interest on that amount at the Interest Rate for the period from the final date for payment until payment is made. Interest under this clause 4·9·5 ~~4·10·6~~ shall be a debt due to the Contractor from ~~by~~ the Employer.

·6̶7̶ Acceptance of a~~ny~~ payment of interest under clause 4·9·5 ~~4·10·6~~ shall not in any circumstances be construed as a waiver of the Contractor's right to proper payment of the principal amount due, to suspend performance under clause 4·11 or to terminate his employment under section 8.

Payment Notices, Pay Less Notices and general provisions

4·10 ·1 Each Payment Notice under this Contract shall specify the sum that the Party giving the notice considers to be or have been due at the due date in respect of the relevant payment and the basis on which that sum has been calculated.

·2 A Pay Less Notice:

·1 (where it is to be given by the Employer) shall specify both the sum that he considers to be due to the Contractor at the date the notice is given and the basis on which that sum has been calculated;

·2 (where it is to be given by the Contractor) shall specify both the sum that he considers to be due to the Employer at the date the notice is given and the basis on which that sum has been calculated.

·3 A Payment Notice or a Pay Less Notice to be given by the Employer may be given on his behalf by the Employer's Agent or by any other person who the Employer notifies the Contractor as being authorised to do so.

·4 In relation to the requirements for the giving of notices under section 4 and the submission of a Final Statement, it is immaterial that the amount then considered to be due may be zero.

·5 Notwithstanding his fiduciary interest in the Retention as stated in clause 4·16, the Employer is entitled to exercise any rights under this Contract of withholding or deduction from sums due or to become due to the Contractor, whether or not any Retention is included in any such sum under clause 4·18.

Contractor's right of suspension

4·11 ·1 Without affecting the Contractor's other rights and remedies, if the Employer, ~~subject to any notice issued pursuant to clause 4·10·4,~~ fails to pay the Contractor the sum payable in accordance with clause 4·9 ~~in full (including~~ together with any VAT properly chargeable in respect of such payment) by the final date for payment ~~as required by these Conditions~~ and the failure continues for 7 days after the Contractor has given notice to the Employer of his intention to suspend the performance of his obligations under this Contract and the ground or grounds on which it is intended to suspend performance, the Contractor may suspend ~~such~~ performance of any or all of his obligations until payment is made in full.

·2 Where the Contractor exercises his right of suspension under clause 4·11·1, he shall be entitled to a reasonable amount in respect of costs and expenses reasonably incurred by him as a result of the exercise of the right.

·3 Applications in respect of any such costs and expenses shall be made to the Employer and the Contractor shall with his application or on request submit such details of the costs and expenses as are reasonably necessary to enable his entitlement to be ascertained.

Final Statement ~~– submission~~ and final payment[44]

4·12 ·1 Following ~~Within 3 months of~~ practical completion of the Works the Contractor shall submit the Final Statement ~~for agreement by~~ to the Employer, and ~~the Contractor shall~~ supply him ~~the Employer~~ with such supporting documents as ~~he~~ the Employer may reasonably require.

·2 The Final Statement shall set out the adjustments to the Contract Sum to be made in accordance with clause 4·2 and shall state:

·1 the Contract Sum, as so adjusted; and

---

[44] The effect of the Final Statement is set out in clause 1·8.

© The Joint Contracts Tribunal Limited 2011

·2 the sum of ~~the~~ amounts already paid by the Employer to the Contractor,

and the final payment shall be ~~with~~ the difference (if any) between the two sums, which shall be shown ~~expressed~~ as a balance due to the Contractor from the Employer or to the Employer from the Contractor, as the case may be. The Final Statement shall state the basis on which that amount has been calculated, including details of all such adjustments.

·3 If the Contractor does not submit the Final Statement within ~~the~~ 3 months of practical completion of the Works, ~~period referred to in clause 4·12·1~~ the Employer may on or after the expiry of that period give ~~notice to~~ the Contractor notice that unless ~~it~~ that statement is submitted ~~by the Contractor~~ within 2 months from the date of the notice the Employer may himself issue a final statement in lieu of that from the Contractor.

·4 Unless the Contractor submits the Final Statement prior to the Employer exercising that right ~~Failing such submission by the Contractor within the notice period~~, the Employer may at any time after the 2 month notice period issue a final statement to the Contractor ('the Employer's Final Statement') in the form and with the details required by clause 4·12·2, so far as the Employer, on the information in his possession, is reasonably able to do so.

·5 The due date for the final payment ~~The Final Statement or, if none is issued prior to expiry of the 2 month notice period, the Employer's Final Statement~~ shall be the date ~~on the expiry of~~ one month after ~~from~~ whichever of the following occurs last:

    ·1 the end of the Rectification Period in respect of the Works or (where there are Sections) the last such period to expire;

    ·2 the date stated in the Notice of Completion of Making Good under clause 2·36 or (where there are Sections) in the last such notice to be issued; or

    ·3 the date of submission to the other Party of the Final Statement ~~to the Employer~~ or, if issued first, ~~(where applicable)~~ the Employer's Final Statement ('the relevant statement'). ~~to the Contractor,~~

·6 ~~be conclusive as to the balance due between the Parties under this Contract e~~Except to the extent that prior to the due date for the final payment ~~expiry of that one month period,~~ the Employer gives notice to the Contractor disputing anything in the Final Statement or the Contractor gives notice to the Employer disputing anything in the Employer's Final Statement, and~~,~~ subject to clause 1·8·2, the relevant statement shall upon the due date become ~~upon becoming~~ conclusive as to the sum due under clause 4·12·2 and ~~that balance, shall~~ have the further effects stated in clause 1·8.

·7~~6~~ The final date for payment shall be 28 days from the due date. Not later than 5 days after the due date ~~Final Statement or Employer's Final Statement becomes conclusive as to the balance due between the Parties in accordance with clause 4·12·5~~, and notwithstanding any dispute regarding the relevant statement, the Party by whom the statement shows the final payment as ~~balance is~~ payable ('the payer ~~paying Party~~') shall give a Payment Notice ~~notice~~ to the other Party with the details specified in clause 4·10·1. ~~which shall, in respect of the balance stated as due, specify the amount of the payment proposed to be made, to what the amount relates and the basis on which the amount has been calculated.~~Subject to any Pay Less Notice under clause 4·12·8, the payment to be made on or before the final date for payment shall be the sum stated in the Payment Notice or, if such notice is not given, the balance stated in the relevant statement.

·8 If the payer intends to pay less than the sum stated in the Payment Notice or, in default of such notice, less than the amount stated in the relevant statement, he shall not later than 5 days before the final date for payment give the other Party a Pay Less Notice in accordance with clause 4·10·2.

·9 Where a Pay Less Notice is given, the payment to be made on or before the final date for payment shall not be less than the amount stated as due in the notice.

·7 ~~The final date for payment of the balance shall be 28 days from the date the Final Statement or Employer's Final Statement becomes conclusive as to the balance due in accordance with clause 4·12·5. Not later than 5 days before the final date for payment of the balance the paying Party may give a notice to the other Party which shall specify any amount proposed to be withheld or deducted from any balance due to the other Party, the ground or grounds for such withholding or deduction and the amount of withholding or deduction attributable to each ground.~~

·8   Where the paying Party does not give a notice pursuant to clause 4·12·6, he shall, subject to any notice given under clause 4·12·7, pay the other Party any balance stated as due to the other Party in the Final Statement or Employer's Final Statement.

·10̶9̶   If the payer paying Party fails properly to pay the final payment balance, or any part of it, by the final date for its payment, he shall, in addition to any unpaid amount that should properly have been paid, the amount not properly paid pay to the other Party simple interest on that amount at the Interest Rate for the period from the final date for payment until payment is made.

·11̶1̶
0̶   Acceptance of a payment of interest under clause 4·12·10̶9̶ shall not in any circumstances be construed as a waiver of any right to proper payment of the principal amount due balance.

·12̶1̶
1̶   The final payment balance due and any interest under this clause 4·12 shall be a debt due from the payer by the paying Party to the other Party.

Gross Valuation

Ascertainment – Alternative A

4·13   The Gross Valuation shall be the total of the amounts referred to in clauses 4·13·1 and 4·13·2 less the total of the amounts referred to in clause 4·13·3, calculated as at completion of the relevant stage.

·1   The following which are subject to Retention shall be included:

·1   the cumulative value at the relevant stage;

·2   the value of any Changes or other work referred to in clause 5·2 that are relevant to the Interim Payment (whether agreed pursuant to clause 5·2 or valued under the Valuation Rules) but excluding any amounts referred to in clause 4·13·2·4̶3̶;

·3   the value of any Listed Items, when their value is to be included under clause 4·15;

·4   the amount of any adjustment under Fluctuations Option C (if applicable);

·5   where Fluctuations Option C is applicable and where in accordance with the Formula Rules amounts in the Value of Work are to be allocated to lift installations, structural steelwork installations or catering equipment installations, the total value of Site Materials of those descriptions, provided that their value shall only be included if they are adequately protected against weather and other casualties and they are not on the Works prematurely; and

·6   the amount of any adjustment by Confirmed Acceptance of an Acceleration Quotation.

·2   The following which are not subject to Retention shall be included:

·1   any amounts to be included in Interim Payments in accordance with clause 4·3 by the Employer as a result of payments made or costs incurred by the Contractor under clause 2·5·2, 2·20, or 3·12, 6·10·2 or 6·10·3 or paragraph A·5·1, B·2·1·2 or C·3·1 of Schedule 3;

·2   any amounts payable under clause 4·11·2;

·3̶2̶   any amounts ascertained under clause 4·20;

·4̶3̶   any amounts in respect of any restoration, replacement or repair of loss or damage and removal and disposal of debris under paragraphs B·3·5 and or C·4·5·2 of Schedule 3 or clause 6·11·5·2 6·10·4·2; and

·5̶4̶   any amount payable to the Contractor under Fluctuations Option A or B, if applicable.

·3   The following shall be deducted:

·1   any amounts deductible under clause 2·35 or 3·6; and

·2   any amount allowable by the Contractor to the Employer under clause 6·10·2 or under Fluctuations Option A or B, if applicable.

Ascertainment – Alternative B

4·14 The Gross Valuation shall be the total of the amounts referred to in clauses 4·14·1 and 4·14·2 less the total of the amounts referred to in clause 4·14·3, calculated as at the date for making an Interim Application under clause 4·8·3.

·1 The total values of the following which are subject to Retention shall be included:

·1 work properly executed including any design work carried out by the Contractor and work so executed for which a value has been agreed pursuant to clause 5·2 or which has been valued under the Valuation Rules, together, where applicable, with any adjustment of that value under Fluctuations Option C or by Confirmed Acceptance of an Acceleration Quotation, but excluding any amounts referred to in clause 4·14·2·43;

·2 Site Materials provided that their value shall only be included if they are adequately protected against weather and other casualties and they are not on the Works prematurely; and

·3 Listed Items (if any), when their value is to be included under clause 4·15.

·2 The following which are not subject to Retention shall be included:

·1 any amounts to be included in Interim Payments in accordance with clause 4·3 by the Employer as a result of payments made or costs incurred by the Contractor under clause 2·5·2, 2·20, 3·12, 6·10·2 or 6·10·3 or 6·16 or paragraph A·5·1, B·2·1·2 or C·3·1 of Schedule 3;

·2 any amounts payable under clause 4·11·2;

·32 any amounts ascertained under clause 4·20;

·43 any amounts in respect of any restoration, replacement or repair of loss or damage and removal and disposal of debris which under paragraphs B·3·5 and or C·4·5·2 of Schedule 3 or clause 6·11·5·2 are treated as a Change; and

·54 any amount payable to the Contractor under Fluctuations Option A or B, if applicable.

·3 The following shall be deducted:

·1 any amounts deductible under clause 2·35 or 3·6; and

·2 any amount allowable by the Contractor to the Employer under clause 6·10·2 or under Fluctuations Option A or B, if applicable.

Off-site materials and goods

4·15 The sum amount stated as due in an Interim Application for Interim Payment shall include the value of any Listed Items before their delivery to or adjacent to the Works provided that the following conditions have been fulfilled:

·1 the Listed Items are in accordance with this Contract;

·2 the Contractor has provided the Employer with reasonable proof that:

·1 the property in the Listed Items is vested in the Contractor; and

·2 the Listed Items are insured against loss or damage for their full value under a policy of insurance protecting the interests of the Employer and the Contractor in respect of the Specified Perils, during the period commencing with the transfer of property in the Listed Items to the Contractor until they are delivered to, or adjacent to, the Works;

·3 at the premises where the Listed Items have been manufactured or assembled or are stored, there is in relation to those items clear identification of:

·1 the Employer as the person to whose order they are held; and

·2 their destination as the Works,

and the items either are set apart or have been clearly and visibly marked, individually or in sets, by letters or figures or by reference to a pre-determined code; and

·4   in the case of uniquely identified Listed Items, the Contractor, if it is stated in the Contract Particulars as required, has provided a bond in favour of the Employer from a surety approved by the Employer[43] in the terms set out in Part 2 of Schedule 6 ('the required bond') in the amount specified in the Contract Particulars for this clause 4·15·4; or

·5   in the case of Listed Items which are not uniquely identified, the Contractor has provided the required bond in the amount specified in the Contract Particulars for this clause 4·15·5.

Retention

Rules on treatment of Retention

4·16   The Retention which the Employer may deduct and retain as referred to in clause 4·7·2·1 4·8·1 shall be subject to the following rules:

·1   the Employer's interest in the Retention is fiduciary as trustee for the Contractor (but without obligation to invest);

·2   except where the Employer is a Local Authority, the Employer shall, to the extent that he exercises his right under clause 4·18 and if the Contractor so requests, shall at the time of each Interim Payment place the Retention in a separate bank account (so designated as to identify the amount as the Retention held by the Employer on trust as provided in clause 4·16·1) and notify the Contractor that the amount has been so placed. The Employer shall be entitled to the full beneficial interest in any interest accruing on the separate bank account and shall be under no duty to account for any such interest to the Contractor.

Retention Bond

4·17   Where the Contract Particulars state that clause 4·17 applies, then:

·1   subject to clauses 4·17·3 and 4·17·4, the provisions of clauses 4·7·2·1 4·8·1 and 4·16 permitting the deduction of the Retention shall not apply[45];

·2   on or before the Date of Possession the Contractor shall provide to the Employer and thereafter maintain a bond ('the Retention Bond') in favour of the Employer from a surety approved by the Employer ('the Surety')[43] in the terms set out in Part 3 of Schedule 6, incorporating in clauses 2 *(maximum aggregate sum)* and 6·3 *(expiry date)* of the bond, the sum and date stated in the Contract Particulars;

·3   if the Contractor fails to provide or maintain the Retention Bond in accordance with clause 4·17·2, the provisions of clauses 4·7·2·1 4·8·1 and 4·16 permitting the deduction of the Retention shall apply in respect of Interim Payments issued after the date of the failure, save that if the Contractor subsequently provides the required bond the Employer shall, in the next Interim Payment to be issued after such compliance, release to the Contractor the Retention deducted during the period of failure;

·4   if at any time the amount of the Retention that would have been deducted had the provisions of clauses 4·7·2·1 4·8·1 and 4·16 applied exceeds the aggregate sum stated in the Retention Bond, then either the Contractor shall arrange with the Surety for the aggregate sum to equate to such amount or the amount not covered by the bond may be deducted as Retention; and

·5   where the Employer has required the Contractor to provide a performance bond, then, in respect of any default for which the Employer is entitled to make a demand under the performance bond as well as under the Retention Bond, the Employer shall first have recourse to the Retention Bond.

---

[45]   In view of the provisions of clauses 4·2 and 4·3 of the form of Retention Bond in Schedule 6, the Employer should keep up-to-date records of the amount of Retention that would have been retained had clauses 4·7·2·1 4·8·1 and 4·16 applied.

Retention – amounts and periods

4·18 The Retention which the Employer may deduct and retain shall be such percentage of the total amount included in the Gross Valuation under clause 4·13·1 or 4·14·1, whichever is applicable, in any Interim Payment as is permitted by ~~arises from the operation of~~ the following rules[46]:

- ·1 the Retention Percentage shall be 3 per cent ~~(~~or such other rate as is stated in the Contract Particulars~~)~~;

- ·2 the Retention Percentage may be deducted from so much of the total amount as relates to:

  - ·1 work where the Works or (where there are Sections) the Section(s) of which it forms part have not reached practical completion; and

  - ·2 Site Materials and Listed Items;

- ·3 half the Retention Percentage may be deducted from so much of the total amount as relates to work where the Works or relevant Section(s) have reached practical completion but in respect of which a Notice of Completion of Making Good under clause 2·36 has not been issued or relates to work in a Relevant Part where ~~or~~ a notice under clause 2·32 has not been issued.

Fluctuations – choice of provisions

4·19 Fluctuations shall be dealt with by the application of Schedule 7 in accordance with whichever of the following is stated in the Contract Particulars to apply:

Fluctuations Option A: contribution, levy and tax fluctuations, or
Fluctuations Option B: labour and materials cost and tax fluctuations, or
Fluctuations Option C: formula adjustment.[47]

Loss and Expense

Matters materially affecting regular progress

4·20 If in the execution of this Contract the Contractor incurs or is likely to incur direct loss and/or expense for which he would not be reimbursed by a payment under any other provision in these Conditions due to a deferment of giving possession of the site or relevant part of it under clause 2·4 or because the regular progress of the Works or of any part of them has been or is likely to be materially affected by any of the Relevant Matters, the Contractor may make an application to the Employer. If the Contractor makes such application, save where these Conditions provide that there shall be no addition to the Contract Sum or otherwise exclude the operation of this clause, the amount of the loss and/or expense which has been or is being incurred shall be ascertained and added to the Contract Sum; provided always that the Contractor shall:

- ·1 make his application as soon as it has become, or should reasonably have become, apparent to him that the regular progress has been or is likely to be affected;

- ·2 in support of his application submit to the Employer upon request such information and details as the Employer may reasonably require.

Relevant Matters

4·21 The following are the Relevant Matters:

- ·1 Changes and any other matters or instructions which under these Conditions are to be treated as, or as requiring, a Change;

- ·2 Employer's instructions:

---

[46] For the effect of clause 4·18·3, see the Design and Build Contract Guide.

[47] Fluctuations Option B should be used where the Parties have agreed to allow the labour and materials cost and tax fluctuations to which paragraphs B·1 to B·3 of that Option refer. Fluctuations Option C should be used where the Parties have agreed that fluctuations should be dealt with by adjustment of the Contract Sum under the JCT Formula Rules.

.1   under clause 3·10 or 3·11; or

.2   for the opening up for inspection or testing of any work, materials or goods under clause 3·12 (including making good), unless the inspection or test shows that the work, materials or goods are not in accordance with this Contract;

.3   compliance with clause 3·15·1 or with Employer's instructions under clause 3·15·2;

.4   ~~suspension by the Contractor under clause 4·11 of the performance of his obligations under this Contract, provided the suspension was not frivolous or vexatious;~~

.4̶5̶   delay in receipt of any permission or approval for the purposes of Development Control Requirements necessary for the Works to be carried out or proceed, which delay the Contractor has taken all practicable steps to avoid or reduce;

.5̶6̶   any impediment, prevention or default, whether by act or omission, by the Employer or any of the Employer's Persons, except to the extent caused or contributed to by any default, whether by act or omission, of the Contractor or of any of the Contractor's Persons.

Amounts ascertained – addition to Contract Sum

4·22   Any amounts from time to time ascertained under clause 4·20 shall be added to the Contract Sum.

Reservation of Contractor's rights and remedies

4·23   The provisions of clauses 4·20 to 4·22 are without prejudice to any other rights and remedies which the Contractor may possess.

General

Definition of Changes

5·1　　The term 'Change' means:

　·1　　a change in the Employer's Requirements which makes necessary the alteration or modification of the design, quality or quantity of the Works, otherwise than such as may be reasonably necessary for the purposes of rectification pursuant to clause 3·13, including:

　　·1　　the addition, omission or substitution of any work;

　　·2　　the alteration of the kind or standard of any of the materials or goods to be used in the Works;

　　·3　　the removal from the site of any work executed or Site Materials other than work, materials or goods which are not in accordance with this Contract;

　·2　　the imposition by the Employer of any obligations or restrictions in regard to the matters set out in this clause 5·1·2 or the addition to or alteration or omission of any such obligations or restrictions so imposed or imposed by the Employer in the Employer's Requirements in regard to:

　　·1　　access to the site or use of any specific parts of the site;

　　·2　　limitations of working space;

　　·3　　limitations of working hours; or

　　·4　　the execution or completion of the work in any specific order.[48]

Valuation of Changes and provisional sum work

5·2　　The value of:

　·1　　all Changes required by Employer's instructions;

　·2　　all work which under these Conditions is to be treated as a Change; and

　·3　　all work executed by the Contractor in accordance with Employer's instructions as to the expenditure of Provisional Sums included in the Employer's Requirements

shall be such amount as is agreed by the Employer and the Contractor or, where not agreed, shall, unless otherwise agreed by the Employer and the Contractor, be the amount valued (a 'Valuation') in accordance with clauses 5·4 to 5·7 ('the Valuation Rules').

Giving effect to Valuations, agreements etc.

5·3　　Effect shall be given by means of addition to or deduction from the Contract Sum to each agreement by the Employer and the Contractor under clause 5·2 and each Valuation.

---

[48]　　See clause 3·5 for the Contractor's right of reasonable objection to Changes.

The Valuation Rules

Measurable Work

5·4   Valuations shall be made in accordance with this clause 5·4 and, so far as is relevant, clauses 5·5 to 5·7.

·1   Allowance shall be made in such Valuations for the addition or omission of the relevant design work.

·2   The valuation of additional or substituted work shall be consistent with the values of work of a similar character set out in the Contract Sum Analysis, making due allowance for any change in the conditions under which work is carried out and/or any significant change in the quantity of the work so set out. Where there is no work of a similar character set out in the Contract Sum Analysis a fair valuation shall be made.

·3   The valuation of the omission of work set out in the Contract Sum Analysis shall be in accordance with the values therein for such work.

·4   Any valuation of work under clauses 5·4·2 and 5·4·3 shall include allowance for any necessary addition to or reduction of the provision of site administration, site facilities and temporary works.

Daywork

5·5   Where the execution of additional or substituted work cannot be valued in accordance with clause 5·4, the Valuation shall comprise:

·1   the prime cost of such work (calculated in accordance with the 'Definition of Prime Cost of Daywork carried out under a Building Contract' issued by The Royal Institution of Chartered Surveyors (RICS) and the Construction Confederation as current at the Base Date) together with Percentage Additions to each section of the prime cost at the rates stated in the document identified in the Contract Particulars or, if they apply in respect of labour, at the All-Inclusive Rates stated in such document; or

·2   where the work is within the province of any specialist trade and the RICS and the appropriate body representing the employers in that trade have agreed and issued a definition of prime cost of daywork[49], the prime cost of such work calculated in accordance with that definition current at the Base Date, together with Percentage Additions on the prime cost at the rates stated in the document identified in the Contract Particulars or, if they apply in respect of labour, at the All-Inclusive Rates stated in such document.

Provided that in any case vouchers specifying the time daily spent upon the work, the workmen's names, the plant and the materials employed shall be delivered for verification to the Employer not later than 7 Business Days after the work has been executed.

Change of conditions for other work

5·6   If as a result of:

·1   compliance with any instruction requiring a Change; or

·2   compliance with any instruction as to the expenditure of a Provisional Sum,

there is a substantial change in the conditions under which any other work is executed, then such other work shall be treated as if it had been the subject of an instruction requiring a Change and shall be valued in accordance with the provisions of this section 5.

---

[49]   There are currently three definitions to which clause 5·5·2 refers, namely those agreed between the RICS and the Electrical Contractors Association, the RICS and the Electrical Contractors Association of Scotland and the RICS and the Heating and Ventilating Contractors Association.

Additional provisions

5·7   ·1   To the extent that a Valuation does not relate to the execution of additional or substituted work or the omission of work or to the extent that the valuation of any work or liabilities directly associated with a Change cannot reasonably be effected in the Valuation by the application of clauses 5·4 to 5·6, a fair valuation shall be made.

·2   No allowance shall be made under the Valuation Rules for any effect upon the regular progress of the Works or of any part of them or for any other direct loss and/or expense for which the Contractor would be reimbursed by payment under any other provision in these Conditions.

Injury to Persons and Property

Liability of Contractor – personal injury or death

6·1   The Contractor shall be liable for, and shall indemnify the Employer against, any expense, liability, loss, claim or proceedings whatsoever in respect of personal injury to or the death of any person arising out of or in the course of or caused by the carrying out of the Works, except to the extent that the same is due to any act or neglect of the Employer, of any of the Employer's Persons or of any Statutory Undertaker.

Liability of Contractor – injury or damage to property

6·2   The Contractor shall be liable for, and shall indemnify the Employer against, any expense, liability, loss, claim or proceedings in respect of any loss, injury or damage whatsoever to any property real or personal in so far as such loss, injury or damage arises out of or in the course of or by reason of the carrying out of the Works and to the extent that the same is due to any negligence, breach of statutory duty, omission or default of the Contractor or of any of the Contractor's Persons. This liability and indemnity is subject to clause 6·3 and, where Insurance Option C (Schedule 3, paragraph C·1) applies, excludes loss or damage to any property required to be insured thereunder caused by a Specified Peril.

Injury or damage to property – Works and Site Materials excluded

6·3   ·1   Subject to clauses 6·3·2 and 6·3·3, the reference in clause 6·2 to 'property real or personal' does not include the Works, work executed and/or Site Materials up to and including whichever is the earlier of:

       ·1   the date of issue of the Practical Completion Statement; or

       ·2   the date of termination of the Contractor's employment.

   ·2   Where a Section Completion Statement is issued in respect of a Section, that Section shall not after the date of issue of that statement be regarded as 'the Works' or 'work executed' for the purpose of clause 6·3·1.

   ·3   If clause 2·30 has been operated, then, after the Relevant Date, the Relevant Part shall not be regarded as 'the Works' or 'work executed' for the purpose of clause 6·3·1.

Insurance against Personal Injury and Property Damage

Contractor's insurance of his liability

6·4   ·1   Without prejudice to his obligation to indemnify the Employer under clauses 6·1 and 6·2, the Contractor shall take out and maintain insurance in respect of claims arising out of his liability referred to in clauses 6·1 and 6·2 which:

       ·1   in respect of claims for personal injury to or the death of any employee of the Contractor arising out of and in the course of such person's employment, shall comply with all relevant legislation; and

       ·2   for all other claims to which clause 6·4·1 applies[50], shall indemnify the Employer in like manner to the Contractor (but only to the extent that the Contractor may be liable to indemnify the Employer under the terms of this Contract) and shall be in a sum not less than that stated in the Contract Particulars for any one occurrence or series of

---

[50]   It should be noted that the cover granted under public liability policies taken out pursuant to clause 6·4·1 may not be co-extensive with the indemnity given to the Employer in clauses 6·1 and 6·2: for example, each claim may be subject to the excess in the policy and cover may not be available in respect of loss or damage due to gradual pollution.

occurrences arising out of one event.[51]

·2 As and when reasonably required to do so by the Employer, the Contractor shall send to the Employer documentary evidence that the insurances required by clause 6·4·1 have been taken out and are being maintained, and at any time the Employer may (but shall not unreasonably or vexatiously) require that the relevant policy or policies and related premium receipts be sent to the Employer for such inspection.

·3 If the Contractor defaults in taking out or in maintaining insurance in accordance with clause 6·4·1 the Employer may himself insure against any liability or expense which he may incur as a result of such default and the amount paid or payable by him in respect of premiums therefor may be deducted from any sums due or to become due to the Contractor under this Contract or shall be recoverable from the Contractor as a debt.

Contractor's insurance of liability of Employer

6·5 ·1 If the Employer's Requirements state that insurance under clause 6·5·1 is required, the Contractor shall take out and maintain a policy of insurance in the names of the Employer and the Contractor[52] for the amount of indemnity stated in the Contract Particulars in respect of any expense, liability, loss, claim or proceedings which the Employer may incur or sustain by reason of injury or damage to any property caused by collapse, subsidence, heave, vibration, weakening or removal of support or lowering of ground water arising out of or in the course of or by reason of the carrying out of the Works, excluding injury or damage:

·1 for which the Contractor is liable under clause 6·2;

·2 which is attributable to errors or omissions in the designing of the Works;

·3 which can reasonably be foreseen to be inevitable having regard to the nature of the work to be executed and the manner of its execution;

·4 (if Insurance Option C applies) which it is the responsibility of the Employer to insure under paragraph C·1 of Schedule 3;

·5 to the Works and Site Materials except where the Practical Completion Statement has been issued or in so far as any Section is the subject of a Section Completion Statement;

·6 which arises from any consequence of war, invasion, act of foreign enemy, hostilities (whether war is declared or not), civil war, rebellion or revolution, insurrection or military or usurped power;

·7 which is directly or indirectly caused by or contributed to by or arises from the Excepted Risks;

·8 which is directly or indirectly caused by or arises out of pollution or contamination of buildings or other structures or of water or land or the atmosphere happening during the period of insurance, save that this exception shall not apply in respect of pollution or contamination caused by a sudden identifiable, unintended and unexpected incident which takes place in its entirety at a specific moment in time and place during the period of insurance (all pollution or contamination which arises out of one incident being considered for the purpose of this insurance to have occurred at the time such incident takes place); or

·9 which results in any costs or expenses being incurred by the Employer or in any other sums being payable by the Employer in respect of damages for breach of contract, except to the extent that such costs or expenses or damages would have attached in the absence of any contract.

·2 Any insurance under clause 6·5·1 shall be placed with insurers approved by the Employer, and the Contractor shall deposit with the Employer the policy or policies and related premium

---

[51] The Contractor may, if he wishes, insure for a sum greater than that stated in the Contract Particulars.

[52] A policy of insurance taken out for the purposes of clause 6·5 should not have an expiry date earlier than the end of the Rectification Period.

receipts.

·3   If the Contractor defaults in taking out or in maintaining the Joint Names Policy as provided in clause 6·5·1 the Employer may himself insure against any risk in respect of which the default shall have occurred and may deduct a sum or sums equivalent to the amount paid or payable in respect of premiums from any sums due or to become due to the Contractor or such amount shall be recoverable by the Employer from the Contractor as a debt.

Excepted Risks

6·6   Notwithstanding clauses 6·1, 6·2 and 6·4·1, the Contractor shall not be liable either to indemnify the Employer or to insure against any personal injury to or the death of any person or any damage, loss or injury to the Works, Site Materials, work executed, the site, or any other property, caused by the effect of an Excepted Risk.

Insurance of the Works

Insurance Options

6·7   Insurance Options A, B and C are set out in Schedule 3. The Insurance Option that applies to this Contract is that stated in the Contract Particulars.[53]

Related definitions

6·8   In Schedule 3 and, so far as relevant, in the clauses of these Conditions the following phrases shall have the meanings given below:

All Risks Insurance[54]:   insurance which provides cover against any physical loss or damage to work executed and Site Materials and against the reasonable cost of the removal and disposal of debris and of any shoring and propping of the Works which results from such physical loss or damage but excluding the cost necessary to repair, replace or rectify:

(a)   property which is defective due to:

(i)   wear and tear,

(ii)   obsolescence, or

(iii)   deterioration, rust or mildew;

(b)   any work executed or any Site Materials lost or damaged as a result

---

[53]   **Insurance Option A** is applicable to the erection of new buildings where the **Contractor** is required to take out a Joint Names Policy for All Risks Insurance for of the Works and **Insurance Option B** is applicable where the **Employer** has elected to take out such that Joint Names Policy. **Insurance Option C** is for use in the case of alterations of or extensions to existing structures; under it, the **Employer** is required to take out a Joint Names Policy for All Risks Insurance for the Works and also a Joint Names Policy to insure the existing structures and their contents owned by him or for which he is responsible against loss or damage by the Specified Perils. Some Employers (e.g. tenants and homeowners) may not be able readily to obtain the Joint Names cover, in particular that under paragraph C·1. If so, Option C should not be stated to apply and consequential amendments may be necessary. See the Design and Build Contract Guide.

[54]   The risks and costs that All Risks Insurance is required to cover are defined by exclusions. Policies issued by insurers are not standardised; the way in which insurance for these risks is expressed varies and in some cases it may not be possible for insurance to be taken out against certain of the risks required to be covered. In the case of Terrorism Cover, where the extension of cover will involve an additional premium and may in certain situations be difficult to effect, the requirement is now expressly limited to Pool Re Cover or such other cover as is agreed and set out in the Contract Particulars. That extension and any other relevant details of Works insurance require discussion and agreement between the Parties and their insurance advisers prior to entering into the Contract. See the Design and Build Contract Guide. Clause 6·8 defines by exclusions the risks that All Risks Insurance is required to cover: the required cover includes loss or damage caused by or arising from terrorism. Policies issued by insurers are not standardised; the way in which insurance for these risks is expressed varies and in some cases it may not be possible for insurance to be taken out against certain of the risks covered by the definition of All Risks Insurance. In particular the Parties should note the potential difficulty with respect to Terrorism Cover. Obtaining Terrorism Cover, so as to comply with the requirements of Insurance Option A, B or C, will involve an additional premium and may in certain situations be difficult to effect. The exclusion of any element from the All Risks Insurance and its 'buy back' requires discussion between the Parties and their insurance advisers; these are matters that need to be arranged between the Parties and those advisers prior to entering into the Contract. See the Design and Build Contract Guide.

of its own defect in design, plan, specification, material or workmanship or any other work executed which is lost or damaged in consequence thereof where such work relied for its support or stability on such work which was defective[55];

(c) loss or damage caused by or arising from:

(i) any consequence of war, invasion, act of foreign enemy, hostilities (whether war be declared or not), civil war, rebellion, revolution, insurrection, military or usurped power, confiscation, commandeering, nationalisation or requisition or loss or destruction of or damage to any property by or under the order of any government *de jure* or *de facto* or public, municipal or local authority,

(ii) disappearance or shortage if such disappearance or shortage is only revealed when an inventory is made or is not traceable to an identifiable event, or

(iii) an Excepted Risk.

Excepted Risks: the risks comprise:

(a) ionising radiations or contamination by radioactivity from any nuclear fuel or from any nuclear waste from the combustion of nuclear fuel, radioactive toxic explosive or other hazardous properties of any explosive nuclear assembly or nuclear component thereof, (other than such risk insofar, but only insofar, as it is included in the Terrorism Cover from time to time required to be taken out and maintained under this Contract);

(b) pressure waves caused by aircraft or other aerial devices travelling at sonic or supersonic speeds.; and

(c) any act of terrorism that is not within the Terrorism Cover from time to time required to be taken out and maintained under this Contract.

Joint Names Policy: a policy of insurance which includes the Employer and the Contractor as composite insured and under which the insurers have no right of recourse against any person named as an insured, or, pursuant to clause 6·9, recognised as an insured thereunder.

Pool Re Cover: such insurance against loss or damage to work executed and Site Materials caused by or resulting from terrorism as is from time to time generally available from insurers who are members of the Pool Reinsurance Company Limited scheme or of any similar successor scheme.[56]

Specified Perils: fire, lightning, explosion, storm, flood, escape of water from any water tank, apparatus or pipe, earthquake, aircraft and other aerial devices or articles dropped therefrom, riot and civil commotion, but excluding Excepted Risks.

---

[55] In any All Risks Insurance policy for the Works, cover should not be reduced by any exclusion in the policy that goes beyond the terms of paragraph (b) in this definition; for example, an exclusion in terms that 'This Policy excludes all loss of or damage to the property insured due to defective design, plan, specification, materials or workmanship' would not be in accordance with the terms of the relevant Insurance Options or that definition. In relation to design defects, wider All Risks cover than that specified may be available to Contractors, though it is not standard. In any policy for All Risks Insurance taken out under Insurance Option A or B or paragraph C·2 of Insurance Option C, cover should not be reduced by the terms of any exclusion written in the policy beyond the terms of paragraph (b) in this definition of All Risks Insurance; thus an exclusion in terms 'This Policy excludes all loss of or damage to the property insured due to defective design, plan, specification, materials or workmanship' would not be in accordance with the terms of those Insurance Options or of that definition. Wider All Risks cover than that specified may be available to Contractors, though it is not standard.

[56] As respects Terrorism Cover and the requirements of Insurance Options A, B and C, see footnote [54] and the Design and Build Contract Guide.

Terrorism Cover:	Pool Re Cover or other insurance against ~~provided by a Joint Names Policy under Insurance Option A, B or C for physical~~ loss or damage to work executed and Site Materials (and/or, for the purposes of clause 6·11·1, to an existing structure and/or its contents) caused by or resulting from terrorism. [56] ~~[57]~~

Sub-contractors – Specified Perils cover under Joint Names All Risks Policies

6·9   ·1   The Contractor, where Insurance Option A applies, and the Employer, where Insurance Option B or C applies, shall ensure that the Joint Names Policy referred to in paragraph A·1, A·3, B·1 or C·2 of Schedule 3 shall either:

    ·1   provide for recognition of each sub-contractor as an insured under the relevant Joint Names Policy; or

    ·2   include a waiver by the relevant insurers of any right of subrogation which they may have against any such sub-contractor

in respect of loss or damage by the Specified Perils to the Works or relevant Section, work executed and Site Materials and that this recognition or waiver shall continue up to and including the date of issue of any statement or other document which states that in relation to the Works, the sub-contractor's works are practically complete or, if earlier, the date of termination of the sub-contractor's employment. Where there are Sections and the sub-contractor's works relate to more than one Section, the recognition or waiver for such sub-contractor shall nevertheless cease in relation to a Section upon the issue of such statement or other document for his work in that Section.

    ·2   The provisions of clause 6·9·1 shall apply also in respect of any Joint Names Policy taken out by the Employer under paragraph A·2, or by the Contractor under paragraph B·2·1·2 or C·3·1·2 of Schedule 3.

Terrorism Cover – policy extensions and premiums

6·10   ·1   To the extent that the Joint Names Policy for the Works and Site Materials excludes (or would otherwise exclude) loss or damage caused by terrorism, the Contractor, where Insurance Option A applies, or the Employer, where Insurance Option B or C applies, shall unless otherwise agreed take out and maintain, either as an extension to the Joint Names Policy or as a separate Joint Names Policy, in the same amount and for the required period of the Joint Names Policy, such Terrorism Cover as is specified in or by the Contract Particulars, subject to clauses 6·10·4 and 6·11.

    ·2   Where Insurance Option A applies and the Contractor is required to take out and maintain Pool Re Cover, the cost of that cover and its renewal shall be deemed to be included in the Contract Sum save that, if at any renewal of the cover there is a variation in the rate on which the premium is based, the Contract Sum shall be adjusted by the net amount of the difference between the premium paid by the Contractor and the premium that would have been paid but for the change in rate.

    ·3   Where Insurance Option A applies and Terrorism Cover other than Pool Re Cover is specified as required, the cost of such other cover and of its renewal shall be added to the Contract Sum.

    ·4   Where Insurance Option A applies and the Employer is a Local Authority, if at any renewal of the Terrorism Cover (of any type) there is an increase in the rate on which the premium is based, he may instruct the Contractor not to renew the Terrorism Cover. If he so instructs, the provisions of clauses 6·11·5·1 and 6·11·5·2 shall apply with effect from the renewal date.

Terrorism Cover – non-availability – Employer's options

6·11 ~~0~~   ·1   If the insurers named in ~~the~~ any Joint Names Policy~~, or (where Insurance Option C applies) the insurers named in either or both such policies,~~ notify either Party that, with effect from a specified date (the 'cessation date'), Terrorism Cover will cease and will no longer be available or will only continue to be available with a reduction in the scope or level of such cover, **the**

---

[57]   ~~As respects this definition, the extent of Terrorism Cover and possible difficulties in complying with the requirements of Insurance Options A, B and C, see footnote [52] and the Design and Build Contract Guide.~~

recipient shall immediately notify the other Party.

·2   The Employer, after receipt of such notification but before the cessation date, shall give notice to the Contractor either:

~~either~~

·1   that, notwithstanding the cessation or reduction in scope or level of Terrorism Cover, the Employer requires that the Works continue to be carried out; or

~~or~~

·2   that on the date stated in the Employer's notice (which shall be a date after the date of the insurers' notification but no later than the cessation date) the Contractor's employment under this Contract shall terminate.

·3   Where Insurance Option A applies and the Employer gives notice under clause 6·11·2·1 requiring continuation of the Works, he may instruct the Contractor to effect and maintain any alternative or additional form of Terrorism Cover then reasonably obtainable by the Contractor; the net additional cost to the Contractor of any such cover and its renewal shall be added to the Contract Sum.

·4~~3~~   If the Employer gives notice of termination under clause 6·11~~10~~·2·2, then upon and from such termination the provisions of clauses 8·12·2 to 8·12·5 (excluding clause 8·12·3·5) shall apply and, notwithstanding any ~~the~~ other provisions of this Contract, no further sum shall become due to the Contractor other than the amounts referred to in clauses 8·12·3·1 to 8·12·3·4 ~~which require any further payment or any release of Retention to the Contractor shall cease to apply~~.

·5~~4~~   If the Employer does not give notice of termination under clause 6·11~~10~~·2·2, then:

·1   if work executed and/or Site Materials suffer physical loss or damage caused by terrorism, the Contractor shall with due diligence restore the damaged work, replace or repair any lost or damaged Site Materials, remove and dispose of any debris and proceed with the carrying out of the Works;

·2   the restoration, replacement or repair of such loss or damage and (when required) the removal and disposal of debris shall be treated as a Change, without deduction of Retention and with no reduction in any amount payable to the Contractor pursuant to this clause 6·11·5·2 ~~6·10·4~~ by reason of any act or neglect of the Contractor or of any sub-contractor which may have contributed to the physical loss or damage; and

·3   (where Insurance Option C applies) the requirement that the Works continue to be carried out shall not be affected by any loss or damage to the existing structures and/or their contents caused by terrorism but not so as thereby to impose any obligation on the Employer to reinstate the existing structures or affect the rights of either Party under paragraph C·4·4 of Schedule 3.

Professional Indemnity Insurance

Obligation to insure

6·12~~11~~   The Contractor shall:

·1   forthwith after this Contract has been entered into, take out (unless he has already done so) a Professional Indemnity insurance policy with limits of indemnity of the types and in amounts not less than those stated in the Contract Particulars[58];

·2   thereafter, provided it is available at commercially reasonable rates, maintain such insurance until the expiry of the period stated in the Contract Particulars from the date of practical completion of the Works; and

---

[58]   See the Design and Build Contract Guide.

·3   as and when reasonably requested to do so by the Employer, produce for inspection documentary evidence that such insurance has been effected and/or is being maintained.

Increased cost and non-availability

6·13~~2~~   If the insurance referred to in clause 6·12~~11~~ ceases to be available at commercially reasonable rates, the Contractor shall immediately give notice to the Employer so that the Contractor and the Employer can discuss the means of best protecting their respective positions in the absence of such insurance.

Joint Fire Code – compliance

Application of clauses

6·14~~3~~   Clauses 6·15~~14~~ to 6·17~~16~~ apply where the Contract Particulars state that the Joint Fire Code applies.

Compliance with Joint Fire Code

6·15~~4~~   The Parties shall comply with the Joint Fire Code and any amendments or revisions to it; the Employer shall ensure such compliance by all Employer's Persons and the Contractor shall ensure such compliance by all Contractor's Persons.

Breach of Joint Fire Code – Remedial Measures

6·16~~5~~ ·1   If a breach of the Joint Fire Code occurs and the insurers under the Joint Names Policy in respect of the Works specify by notice to the Employer or the Contractor the remedial measures they require (the 'Remedial Measures'), the Party receiving the notice shall copy it to the other and the Contractor shall ensure that the Remedial Measures are carried out.

·2   If the Contractor, within 7 days of receipt of a notice specifying Remedial Measures, does not begin to carry out or thereafter fails without reasonable cause regularly and diligently to proceed with the Remedial Measures, then the Employer may employ and pay other persons to carry out those Remedial Measures. The Contractor shall be liable for all additional costs incurred by the Employer in connection with such employment and an appropriate deduction shall be made from the Contract Sum.

Joint Fire Code – amendments/revisions

6·17~~6~~   Where the Joint Fire Code is, under the Joint Names Policy, applicable to the Works and amendments or revisions are made to it after the Base Date, the cost, if any, of compliance by the Contractor with amendments or revisions made after that date shall be borne as stated in the Contract Particulars. If the cost is to be borne by the Employer, it shall be added to the Contract Sum.

Assignment

General

7·1 Subject to clause 7·2, neither the Employer nor the Contractor shall without the consent of the other assign this Contract or any rights thereunder.

Rights of enforcement

7·2 Where clause 7·2 is stated in the Contract Particulars to apply, then, in the event of transfer by the Employer of his freehold or leasehold interest in, or of a grant by the Employer of a leasehold interest in, the whole of the premises comprising the Works or (if the Contract Particulars so state) any Section, the Employer may at any time after practical completion of the Works or of the relevant Section grant or assign to any such transferee or lessee the right to bring proceedings in the name of the Employer (whether by arbitration or litigation, whichever applies under this Contract) to enforce any of the terms of this Contract made for the benefit of the Employer. The assignee shall be estopped from disputing any enforceable agreements reached between the Employer and the Contractor which arise out of and relate to this Contract (whether or not they are or appear to be a derogation from the right assigned) and which are made prior to the date of any grant or assignment.

Clauses 7A to 7E – Preliminary

Notices

7·3 Each notice referred to in clauses 7A to 7E shall be given to the Contractor in accordance with clause 1·7·4. In the case of any consultant's collateral warranty other than a specified JCT Collateral Warranty a copy of the warranty shall accompany the notice.

Execution of Collateral Warranties

7·4 Where this Contract is executed as a deed, any collateral warranty to be entered into or procured pursuant to this section 7 shall be executed as a deed. Where this Contract is executed under hand, any such warranty may be executed under hand.

Third Party Rights from Contractor

Rights for Purchasers and Tenants

7A   ·1   Where clause 7A is stated in Part 2 of the Contract Particulars to apply to a Purchaser or Tenant, P&T Rights shall vest in that Purchaser or Tenant on the date of receipt by the Contractor of the Employer's notice to that effect, stating the name of the Purchaser or Tenant and the nature of his interest in the Works.

  ·2   The rights of the Employer and/or the Contractor:

    ·1   to terminate the Contractor's employment under this Contract (whether under section 8 or otherwise), or to agree to rescind this Contract;

    ·2   to agree to amend or otherwise vary or to waive any terms of this Contract;

    ·3   to agree to settle any dispute or other matter arising out of or in connection with this Contract, in each case in or on such terms as they shall in their absolute discretion think fit,

   shall not be subject to the consent of any Purchaser or Tenant.

  ·3   Where P&T Rights have vested in any Purchaser or Tenant, then, notwithstanding the provisions of clause 7A·2, the Employer and the Contractor shall not be entitled without the consent of such Purchaser or Tenant to amend or vary the express provisions of this clause

7A or of Part 1 of Schedule 5 (Third Party Rights for Purchasers and Tenants).

Rights for a Funder

7B ·1 Where clause 7B is stated in Part 2 of the Contract Particulars to apply to a Funder, the Employer may by notice to the Contractor confer Funder Rights on the Funder identified in the notice. Those rights shall vest in the Funder on the date of receipt by the Contractor of the Employer's notice.

·2 Where Funder Rights have been vested in the Funder pursuant to clause 7B·1:

·1 no amendment or variation shall be made to the express terms of this clause 7B or of Part 2 of Schedule 5 (Third Party Rights for a Funder) without the prior written consent of the Funder; and

·2 neither the Employer nor the Contractor shall agree to rescind this Contract, and the rights of the Contractor to terminate his employment under this Contract or to treat it as repudiated shall in all respects be subject to the provisions of paragraph 6 of Part 2 of Schedule 5

but, subject thereto, unless and until the Funder gives notice under paragraph 5 or paragraph 6·4 of Part 2 of Schedule 5, the Contractor shall remain free without the consent of the Funder to agree with the Employer to amend or otherwise vary or to waive any term of this Contract and to settle any dispute or other matter arising out of or in connection with this Contract, in each case in such terms as they think fit, without any requirement that the Contractor obtain the consent of the Funder.

Collateral Warranties

Contractor's Warranties – Purchasers and Tenants

7C Where clause 7C is stated in Part 2 of the Contract Particulars to apply to a Purchaser or Tenant, the Employer may by notice to the Contractor, identifying the Purchaser or Tenant and his interest in the Works, require that the Contractor within 14 days from receipt of that notice enter into with such Purchaser or Tenant a Collateral Warranty in the form CWa/P&T, completed in accordance with the P&T Rights Particulars.

Contractor's Warranty – Funder

7D Where clause 7D is stated in Part 2 of the Contract Particulars to apply to a Funder, the Employer may by notice to the Contractor require that the Contractor within 14 days from receipt of the Employer's notice enter into a Collateral Warranty with the Funder in the form CWa/F, completed in accordance with the Funder Rights Particulars.

Sub-Contractors' Warranties

7E Where Part 2 of the Contract Particulars provides for the giving by any sub-contractor of a Collateral Warranty to a Purchaser, Tenant or Funder or to the Employer, the Contractor shall within 21 days from receipt of the Employer's notice, identifying the relevant sub-contractor, type of warranty and beneficiary, comply with the Contract Documents as to obtaining such warranties in the form SCWa/P&T, SCWa/F or SCWa/E (as the case may be) or such other form as is required for consultants, completed in accordance with Part 2 of the Contract Particulars and subject to any amendments proposed by any such sub-contractor and approved by the Contractor and the Employer, such approval not to be unreasonably delayed or withheld.

General

Meaning of insolvency

8·1 For the purposes of these Conditions, ~~a Party is Insolvent if~~:

·1 a Party which is a company becomes Insolvent:

　·1 when it enters administration within the meaning of Schedule B1 to the Insolvency Act 1986;

　·2 on the appointment of an administrative receiver or a receiver or manager of its property under Chapter I of Part III of that Act, or the appointment of a receiver under Chapter II of that Part;

　·3 on the passing of a resolution for voluntary winding-up without a declaration of solvency under section 89 of that Act; or

　·4 on the making of a winding-up order under Part IV or V of that Act.

·2 a Party which is a partnership becomes Insolvent:

　·1 on the making of a winding-up order against it under any provision of the Insolvency Act 1986 as applied by an order under section 420 of that Act; or

　·2 when sequestration is awarded on the estate of the partnership under section 12 of the Bankruptcy (Scotland) Act 1985 or the partnership grants a trust deed for its creditors.

·3 a Party who is an individual becomes Insolvent:

　·1 on the making of a bankruptcy order against him under Part IX of the Insolvency Act 1986; or

　·2 on the sequestration of his estate under the Bankruptcy (Scotland) Act 1985 or when he grants a trust deed for his creditors.

·4 a Party also becomes Insolvent if:

　·1 he enters into an arrangement, compromise or composition in satisfaction of his debts (excluding a scheme of arrangement as a solvent company for the purposes of amalgamation or reconstruction); or

　·2 (in the case of a Party which is a partnership) each partner is the subject of an individual arrangement or any other event or proceedings referred to in this clause 8·1.

Each of clauses 8·1·1 to 8·1·4 also includes any analogous arrangement, event or proceedings in any other jurisdiction.

·1 ~~he enters into an arrangement, compromise or composition in satisfaction of his debts (excluding a scheme of arrangement as a solvent company for the purposes of amalgamation or reconstruction); or~~

·2 ~~without a declaration of solvency, he passes a resolution or makes a determination that he be wound up; or~~

·3 ~~he has a winding up order or bankruptcy order made against him; or~~

·4 ~~he has appointed to him an administrator or administrative receiver; or~~

·5 ~~he is the subject of any analogous arrangement, event or proceedings in any other jurisdiction; or~~

Notices under section 8

8·2 ·1   Notice of termination of the Contractor's employment shall not be given unreasonably or vexatiously.

·2   Such termination shall take effect on receipt of the relevant notice.

·3   Each notice referred to in this section shall be given in accordance with clause 1·7·4.

Other rights, reinstatement

8·3 ·1   The provisions of clauses 8·4 to 8·7 are without prejudice to any other rights and remedies of the Employer. The provisions of clauses 8·9 and 8·10 and (in the case of termination under either of those clauses) the provisions of clause 8·12, are without prejudice to any other rights and remedies of the Contractor.

·2   Irrespective of the grounds of termination, the Contractor's employment may at any time be reinstated if and on such terms as the Parties agree.

Termination by Employer

Default by Contractor

8·4 ·1   If, before practical completion of the Works, the Contractor:

·1   without reasonable cause wholly or substantially suspends the carrying out of the Works; or

·2   fails to proceed regularly and diligently with the performance of his obligations under this Contract; or

·3   refuses or neglects to comply with a notice or instruction from the Employer requiring him to remove any work, materials or goods not in accordance with this Contract and by such refusal or neglect the Works are materially affected; or

·4   fails to comply with clause 3·3 or 7·1; or

·5   fails to comply with clause 3·16,

the Employer may give to the Contractor a notice specifying the default or defaults (the 'specified default or defaults').

·2   If the Contractor continues a specified default for 14 days from receipt of the notice under clause 8·4·1, the Employer may on, or within 21 days from, the expiry of that 14 day period by a further notice to the Contractor terminate the Contractor's employment under this Contract.

·3   If the Employer does not give the further notice referred to in clause 8·4·2 (whether as a result of the ending of any specified default or otherwise) but the Contractor repeats a specified default (whether previously repeated or not), then, upon or within a reasonable time after such repetition, the Employer may by notice to the Contractor terminate that employment.

Insolvency of Contractor

8·5 ·1   If the Contractor is Insolvent, the Employer may at any time by notice to the Contractor terminate the Contractor's employment under this Contract.

·2   The Contractor shall immediately notify the Employer if he makes any proposal, gives notice of any meeting or becomes the subject of any proceedings or appointment relating to any of the matters referred to in clause 8·1.

·3   As from the date the Contractor becomes Insolvent, whether or not the Employer has given such notice of termination:

·1   ~~the provisions of~~ clauses 8·7·3 to ~~8·7·4,~~ 8·7·5 and (if relevant) clause 8·8 shall apply as if such notice had been given ~~and the other provisions of this Contract which require any further payment or any release of Retention shall cease to apply~~;

·2   the Contractor's obligations under Article 1 and these Conditions to carry out and complete the Works shall be suspended; and

·3   the Employer may take reasonable measures to ensure that the site, the Works and Site Materials are adequately protected and that such Site Materials are retained on site; the Contractor shall allow and shall not hinder or delay the taking of those measures.

Corruption

8·6   The Employer shall be entitled by notice to the Contractor to terminate the Contractor's employment, under this or any other contract with the Employer if, in relation to this or any other such contract, the Contractor or any person employed by him or acting on his behalf shall have committed an offence under the Bribery Act 2010 ~~Prevention of Corruption Acts 1889 to 1916~~, or, where the Employer is a Local Authority, shall have given any fee or reward the receipt of which is an offence under sub-section (2) of section 117 of the Local Government Act 1972.

Consequences of termination under clauses 8·4 to 8·6

8·7   If the Contractor's employment is terminated under clause 8·4, 8·5 or 8·6:

·1   the Employer may employ and pay other persons to carry out and complete the Works and to make good any defects of the kind referred to in clause 2·35, and he and they may enter upon and take possession of the site and the Works and (subject to obtaining any necessary third party consents) may use all temporary buildings, plant, tools, equipment and Site Materials for those purposes;

·2   the Contractor shall:

  ·1   when required in writing by the Employer to do so (but not before), remove or procure the removal from the Works of any temporary buildings, plant, tools, equipment, goods and materials belonging to the Contractor or Contractor's Persons;

  ·2   provide the Employer with copies of all Contractor's Design Documents then prepared, whether or not previously provided;

  ·3   if so required by the Employer within 14 days of the date of termination, assign (so far as assignable and so far as he may lawfully be required to do so) to the Employer, without charge, the benefit of any agreement for the supply of materials or goods and/or for the execution of any work for the purposes of this Contract[59];

·3   ~~(if not already applicable) clauses 8·7·4, 8·7·5 and 8·8 shall thereupon apply and the other provisions of this Contract which require any further payment or any release of Retention to the Contractor shall cease to apply;~~

·3   no further sum shall become due to the Contractor under this Contract other than any amount that may become due to him under clause 8·7·5 or 8·8·2 and the Employer need not pay any sum that has already become due either:

  ·1   insofar as the Employer has given or gives a Pay Less Notice under clause 4·9·4; or

  ·2   if the Contractor, after the last date upon which such notice could have been given by the Employer in respect of that sum, has become insolvent within the meaning of clauses 8·1·1 to 8·1·3;

·4   ~~within a reasonable time after~~ following the completion of the Works and the making good of defects in them (or of instructions otherwise, as referred to in clause 2·35), an account of the following shall ~~within 3 months thereafter~~ be set out in a statement prepared by the Employer:

  ·1   the amount of expenses properly incurred by the Employer, including those incurred pursuant to clause 8·7·1 and, where applicable, clause 8·5·3·3, and of any direct loss

---

[59]   Clause 8·7·2·3 may not be effectual in cases of Contractor's insolvency.

and/or damage caused to the Employer and for which the Contractor is liable, whether arising as a result of the termination or otherwise;

·2 the amount of payments made to the Contractor; and

·3 the total amount which would have been payable for the Works in accordance with this Contract;

·5 if the sum of the amounts stated under clauses 8·7·4·1 and 8·7·4·2 exceeds the amount stated under clause 8·7·4·3, the difference shall be a debt payable by the Contractor to the Employer or, if that sum is less, by the Employer to the Contractor.

Employer's decision not to complete the Works

8·8 ·1 If within the period of 6 months from the date of termination of the Contractor's employment the Employer decides not to have the Works carried out and completed, he shall forthwith notify the Contractor. Within a reasonable time from the date of such notification, or if no notification is given but within that 6 month period the Employer does not commence to make arrangements for such carrying out and completion, then upon within 2 months of the expiry of that 6 month period, the Employer shall send to the Contractor a statement setting out:

·1 the total value of work properly executed at the date of termination or date on which the Contractor became Insolvent, ascertained in accordance with these Conditions as if that employment had not been terminated, together with any amounts due to the Contractor under these Conditions not included in such total value; and

·2 the aggregate amount of any expenses properly incurred by the Employer and of any direct loss and/or damage caused to the Employer and for which the Contractor is liable, whether arising as a result of the termination or otherwise.

·2 After taking into account amounts previously paid to the Contractor under this Contract, if the amount stated under clause 8·8·1·2 exceeds the amount stated under clause 8·8·1·1, the difference shall be a debt payable by the Contractor to the Employer or, if the clause 8·8·1·2 amount is less, by the Employer to the Contractor.

Termination by Contractor

Default by Employer

8·9 ·1 If the Employer:

·1 does not pay by the final date for payment the amount properly due to the Contractor in accordance with clause 4·9 respect of any Application for Payment and/or any VAT properly chargeable on that amount; or

·2 fails to comply with clause 7·1; or

·3 fails to comply with clause 3·16,

the Contractor may give to the Employer a notice specifying the default or defaults (the 'specified default or defaults').

·2 If after the Date of Possession (or after any deferred Date of Possession pursuant to clause 2·4) but before practical completion of the Works the carrying out of the whole or substantially the whole of the uncompleted Works is suspended for a continuous period of the length stated in the Contract Particulars by reason of any impediment, prevention or default, whether by act or omission, by the Employer or any of the Employer's Persons, then, unless it is caused by the negligence or default of the Contractor or of any of the Contractor's Persons, the Contractor may give to the Employer a notice specifying the event or events (the 'specified suspension event or events').

·3 If a specified default or a specified suspension event continues for 14 days from the receipt of notice under clause 8·9·1 or 8·9·2, the Contractor may on, or within 21 days from, the expiry of that 14 day period by a further notice to the Employer terminate the Contractor's employment under this Contract.

·4 If the Contractor for any reason does not give the further notice referred to in clause 8·9·3, but (whether previously repeated or not):

> ·1 the Employer repeats a specified default; or
>
> ·2 a specified suspension event is repeated for any period, such that the regular progress of the Works is or is likely to be materially affected thereby,

then, upon or within a reasonable time after such repetition, the Contractor may by notice to the Employer terminate the Contractor's employment under this Contract.

Insolvency of Employer

8·10 ·1 If the Employer is Insolvent, the Contractor may by notice to the Employer terminate the Contractor's employment under this Contract;

·2 the Employer shall immediately notify the Contractor if he makes any proposal, gives notice of any meeting or becomes the subject of any proceedings or appointment relating to any of the matters referred to in clause 8·1;

·3 as from the date the Employer becomes Insolvent, the Contractor's obligations under Article 1 and these Conditions to carry out and complete the Works shall be suspended.

Termination by either Party

8·11 ·1 If, before practical completion of the Works, the carrying out of the whole or substantially the whole of the uncompleted Works is suspended for the relevant continuous period of the length stated in the Contract Particulars by reason of one or more of the following events:

> ·1 force majeure;
>
> ·2 Employer's instructions under clause 2·13, 3·9 or 3·10 issued as a result of the negligence or default of any Statutory Undertaker;
>
> ·3 loss or damage to the Works occasioned by any of the Specified Perils;
>
> ·4 civil commotion or the use or threat of terrorism and/or the activities of the relevant authorities in dealing with such event or threat;
>
> ·5 the exercise by the United Kingdom Government of any statutory power which directly affects the execution of the Works; or
>
> ·6 delay in receipt of any permission or approval for the purposes of Development Control Requirements necessary for the Works to be carried out or proceed, which delay the Contractor has taken all practicable steps to avoid or reduce,

then either Party, subject to clause 8·11·2, may upon the expiry of that relevant period of suspension give notice to the other that, unless the suspension ceases within 7 days after the date of receipt of that notice, he may terminate the Contractor's employment under this Contract. Failing such cessation within that 7 day period, he may then by further notice terminate that employment.

·2 The Contractor shall not be entitled to give notice under clause 8·11·1 in respect of the matter referred to in clause 8·11·1·3 where the loss or damage to the Works occasioned by a Specified Peril was caused by the negligence or default of the Contractor or of any of the Contractor's Persons.

Consequences of Termination under clauses 8·9 to 8·11, etc.

8·12 If the Contractor's employment is terminated under any of clauses 8·9 to 8·11, under clause 6·11~~10·2·2~~ or under paragraph C·4·4 of Schedule 3:

·1 no further sums shall become due to the Contractor otherwise than in accordance with this clause 8·12~~the provisions of this clause 8·12 shall thereupon apply and the other provisions of this Contract which require any further payment or any release of Retention to the Contractor shall cease to apply~~;

·2   the Contractor shall:

    ·1   with all reasonable dispatch, remove or procure the removal from the site of any temporary buildings, plant, tools and equipment belonging to the Contractor and Contractor's Persons and, subject to the provisions of clause 8·12·5, all goods and materials (including Site Materials); and

    ·2   provide to the Employer copies of the documents referred to in clause 2·37 then prepared;

·3   where the Contractor's employment is terminated under clause 8·9 or 8·10, the Contractor shall as soon as reasonably practicable prepare and submit an account or, where terminated under clause 8·11 or 6·11~~10~~·2·2 or under paragraph C·4·4 of Schedule 3, the Contractor shall at the Employer's option either prepare and submit that account or, not later than 2 months after the date of termination, provide the Employer with all documents necessary for the Employer to do so, which the Employer shall do with reasonable dispatch (and in any event within 3 months of receipt of such documents). The account shall set out the amounts referred to in clauses 8·12·3·1 to 8·12·3·4 and, if applicable, clause 8·12·3·5, namely:

    ·1   the total value of work properly executed at, and of any design work properly carried out before, the date of termination of the Contractor's employment, ascertained in accordance with these Conditions as if the employment had not been terminated, together with any other amounts due to the Contractor under these Conditions;

    ·2   any sums ascertained in respect of direct loss and/or expense under clause 4·20 (whether ascertained before or after the date of termination);

    ·3   the reasonable cost of removal under clause 8·12·2;

    ·4   the cost of materials or goods (including Site Materials) properly ordered for the Works for which the Contractor then has paid or is legally bound to pay;

    ·5   any direct loss and/or damage caused to the Contractor by the termination;

·4   the account shall include the amount, if any, referred to in clause 8·12·3·5 only where the Contractor's employment is terminated either:

    ·1   under clause 8·9 or 8·10; or

    ·2   under clause 8·11·1·3, if the loss or damage to the Works occasioned by any of the Specified Perils was caused by the negligence or default of the Employer or of any of the Employer's Persons;

·5   after taking into account amounts previously paid to the Contractor under this Contract, the Employer shall pay to the Contractor (or vice versa) the amount properly due in respect of the account within 28 days of its submission to the other Party, without deduction of any Retention. Payment by the Employer for any such materials and goods as are referred to in clause 8·12·3·4 shall be subject to such materials and goods thereupon becoming the Employer's property.

Mediation

9·1   Subject to Article 7, if a dispute or difference arises under this Contract which cannot be resolved by direct negotiations, each Party shall give serious consideration to any request by the other to refer the matter to mediation.[60]

Adjudication

9·2   If a dispute or difference arises under this Contract which either Party wishes to refer to adjudication, the Scheme shall apply, subject to the following:

·1   for the purposes of the Scheme the Adjudicator shall be the person (if any) and the nominating body shall be that stated in the Contract Particulars;

·2   where the dispute or difference is or includes a dispute or difference relating to clause 3·13·3 and as to whether an instruction issued thereunder is reasonable in all the circumstances:

·1   the Adjudicator to decide such dispute or difference shall (where practicable) be an individual with appropriate expertise and experience in the specialist area or discipline relevant to the instruction or issue in dispute;

·2   if the Adjudicator does not have the appropriate expertise and experience, the Adjudicator shall appoint an independent expert with such expertise and experience to advise and report in writing on whether or not the instruction under clause 3·13·3 is reasonable in all the circumstances.

Arbitration

Conduct of arbitration

9·3   Any arbitration pursuant to Article 8 shall be conducted in accordance with the JCT ~~2005~~ 2011 edition of the Construction Industry Model Arbitration Rules (CIMAR), provided that if any amendments to that edition of the Rules have been issued by the JCT the Parties may, by a joint notice in writing to the Arbitrator, state that they wish the arbitration to be conducted in accordance with the Rules as so amended. References in clause 9·4 to a Rule or Rules are references to such Rule(s) as set out in the JCT ~~2005~~ 2011 edition of CIMAR.[61]

Notice of reference to arbitration

9·4   ·1   Where pursuant to Article 8 either Party requires a dispute or difference to be referred to arbitration, that Party shall serve on the other Party a notice of arbitration to such effect in accordance with Rule 2.1 identifying the dispute and requiring the other Party to agree to the appointment of an arbitrator. The Arbitrator shall be an individual agreed by the Parties or, failing such agreement within 14 days (or any agreed extension of that period) after the notice of arbitration is served, appointed on the application of either Party in accordance with Rule 2.3 by the person named in the Contract Particulars.

·2   Where two or more related arbitral proceedings in respect of the Works fall under separate arbitration agreements, Rules 2.6, 2.7 and 2.8 shall apply.

---

[60]   See the Design and Build Contract Guide.

[61]   Arbitration or legal proceedings are **not** an appeal against the decision of the Adjudicator but are a consideration of the dispute or difference as if no decision had been made by an Adjudicator.

·3   After an arbitrator has been appointed either Party may give a further notice of arbitration to the other Party and to the Arbitrator referring any other dispute which falls under Article 8 to be decided in the arbitral proceedings and Rule 3.3 shall apply.

Powers of Arbitrator

9·5   Subject to the provisions of Article 8 and clause 1·8, the Arbitrator shall, without prejudice to the generality of his powers, have power to rectify this Contract so that it accurately reflects the true agreement made by the Parties, to direct such measurements and/or valuations as may in his opinion be desirable in order to determine the rights of the Parties and to ascertain and award any sum which ought to have been the subject of or included in any payment and to open up, review and revise any account, opinion, decision, requirement or notice and to determine all matters in dispute which shall be submitted to him in the same manner as if no such account, opinion, decision, requirement or notice had been given.

Effect of award

9·6   Subject to clause 9·7 the award of the Arbitrator shall be final and binding on the Parties.

Appeal – questions of law

9·7   The Parties hereby agree pursuant to section 45(2)(a) and section 69(2)(a) of the Arbitration Act 1996 that either Party may (upon notice to the other Party and to the Arbitrator):

·1   apply to the courts to determine any question of law arising in the course of the reference; and

·2   appeal to the courts on any question of law arising out of an award made in an arbitration under this arbitration agreement.

Arbitration Act 1996

9·8   The provisions of the Arbitration Act 1996 shall apply to any arbitration under this Contract wherever the same, or any part of it, shall be conducted.

Schedules

Schedule 1   Contractor's Design Submission Procedure
(Clause 2·8)

1   The Contractor shall prepare and submit each of the Contractor's Design Documents to the Employer by the means and in the format stated in the Employer's Requirements or the Contractor's Proposals and in sufficient time to allow any comments of the Employer to be incorporated prior to the relevant Contractor's Design Document being used for procurement and/or in the carrying out of the Works. Where the means and format are not so stated, then, unless and until otherwise agreed with the Employer, the Contractor shall submit 2 copies of each of the Contractor's Design Documents to him.

2   Within 14 days from the date of receipt of any Contractor's Design Document, or (if later) 14 days from either the date or expiry of the period for submission of the same stated in the Contract Documents, the Employer shall return one copy of that Contractor's Design Document to the Contractor marked 'A', 'B' or 'C' provided that a document shall be marked 'B' or 'C' only where the Employer considers that it is not in accordance with this Contract.

3   If the Employer does not respond to a Contractor's Design Document in the time stated in paragraph 2, it shall be regarded as marked 'A'.

4   Where the Employer marks a Contractor's Design Document 'B' or 'C', he shall identify by means of a written comment why he considers that it is not in accordance with this Contract.

5   When a Contractor's Design Document is returned by the Employer:

    ·1   if it is marked 'A', the Contractor shall carry out the Works in strict accordance with that document;

    ·2   if it is marked 'B', the Contractor may carry out the Works in accordance with that document, provided that the Employer's comments are incorporated into it and an amended copy of it is promptly submitted to the Employer; or

    ·3   if it is marked 'C', the Contractor shall take due account of the Employer's comments on it and shall either forthwith resubmit it to the Employer in amended form for comment in accordance with paragraph 1 or notify the Employer under paragraph 7.

6   The Contractor shall not carry out any work in accordance with a Contractor's Design Document marked 'C' and the Employer shall not be liable to pay for any work within the Works executed otherwise than in accordance with Contractor's Design Documents marked 'A' or 'B'.

7   If the Contractor disagrees with a comment of the Employer and considers that the Contractor's Design Document in question is in accordance with this Contract, he shall within 7 days of receipt of the comment notify the Employer that he considers that compliance with the comment would give rise to a Change. Such notification shall be accompanied by a statement setting out the Contractor's reasons. Upon receipt of such a notification the Employer shall within 7 days either confirm or withdraw the comment and, where the comment is confirmed, the Contractor shall amend and resubmit the document accordingly.

8   Provided always that:

    ·1   confirmation or withdrawal of a comment in accordance with paragraph 7 shall not signify acceptance by the Employer that the relevant Contractor's Design Document or amended document is in accordance with this Contract or that compliance with the Employer's comment would give rise to a Change;

·2   where in relation to a comment by the Employer the Contractor does not notify him in accordance with paragraph 7, the comment in question shall not be treated as giving rise to a Change; and

·3   neither compliance with the design submission procedure in this Schedule nor with the Employer's comments shall diminish the Contractor's obligations to ensure that the Contractor's Design Documents and Works are in accordance with this Contract.

Part 1

Each provision applies only if so stated in the Contract Particulars.

Site Manager

1 ·1 Where this paragraph applies, it shall apply in place of clause 3·2 (*Person-in-charge*).

·2 The Contractor shall, prior to the commencement of the Works on the site, appoint a Manager to whose appointment the Employer shall have consented, to act as the full-time representative of the Contractor on the site in charge of the Works. The Contractor shall not remove or replace the Manager so appointed without the Employer's consent, which consent shall not be unreasonably delayed or withheld, and any instructions given to the Manager so appointed shall be deemed to have been issued to the Contractor.

·3 As and when reasonably requested to do so by the Employer the Manager referred to in paragraph 1·2 and such other of the Contractor's Persons as may from time to time be necessary shall attend meetings convened by the Employer in connection with the Works.

·4 The Manager shall keep complete and accurate records in accordance with any provisions relating thereto in the Employer's Requirements and shall make the same available for inspection by the Employer and/or the Employer's Agent at all reasonable times.

Named Sub-Contractors

2 ·1 Where the Employer's Requirements state that work ('Named Sub-Contract Work') is to be executed by a named person who is to be employed by the Contractor as a sub-contractor ('Named Sub-Contractor'):

·1 as soon as reasonably practicable after entering into this Contract the Contractor shall enter into a sub-contract with the Named Sub-Contractor and notify the Employer of the date of such sub-contract;

·2 if the Contractor is unable to enter into a sub-contract with the Named Sub-Contractor he shall immediately inform the Employer of the reason for such inability and provided that reason is bona fide the Employer shall either:

·1 remove the reason for the inability so that the Contractor can enter into the sub-contract by a Change which amends the relevant item in the Employer's Requirements; or

·2 omit by a Change the Named Sub-Contract Work from the Employer's Requirements and issue instructions as to the execution of that work;

the relevant provisions of clause 5·2 (*Valuation of Changes*), clauses 2·23 to 2·26 (*Adjustment of Completion Date*) and clauses 4·20 to 4·23 (*Loss and Expense*) shall apply to any Change issued under paragraph 2·1·2;

·3 the Change referred to in paragraph 2·1·2·2 shall not include any requirement for the work to be executed by a person named in the Change instruction but may require the Contractor to select another person to carry out the work subject to the Employer's consent to the person so selected which consent shall not be unreasonably delayed or withheld;

·4 the Change referred to in paragraph 2·1·2·2 may provide that the work is to be executed by a person to whom clause 2·6 refers (the Employer himself or persons employed or otherwise engaged by him);

·5   if the Contractor wishes to terminate the Named Sub-Contractor's employment for some default, whether by act or omission, by the Named Sub-Contractor he shall first obtain the Employer's consent, which consent shall not be unreasonably delayed or withheld;

·6   if the Named Sub-Contractor's employment is terminated the Contractor shall himself complete any balance of the Named Sub-Contract Work left uncompleted at the date of termination. Such completion shall be treated as a Change except where the termination has resulted from the default, whether by act or omission, of the Contractor, or, where paragraph 2·1·5 applies, the Employer's consent has not been obtained as required by that paragraph;

·7   the Contractor shall account to the Employer for any amounts which he has recovered, or which he could by reasonable diligence have recovered, from the Named Sub-Contractor in respect of the termination as legally due to the Contractor, and which can properly and fairly be regarded as due to the Employer in reduction of the cost to the Employer of the Change;

·8   the Contractor shall include in the Named Sub-Contract conditions a provision which states that the Named Sub-Contractor, having had notice of the terms in paragraph 2 of this Schedule 2, undertakes not to contend, whether in proceedings or otherwise, that the Contractor has suffered or incurred no loss and/or expense or that his liability to the Contractor should be in any way reduced or extinguished by reason of paragraph 2 and in particular paragraph 2·1·6.

·2   The Contractor shall remain wholly responsible for carrying out and completing the Works in all respects in accordance with clause 2·1 notwithstanding that the Employer's Requirements state that work (Named Sub-Contract Work) is to be executed by a named person to which the provisions of paragraph 2 apply.

Bills of Quantities

3   If the Works are described in the Employer's Requirements by Bills of Quantities ('Bills') prepared by or under the direction of the Employer:

·1   the Employer's Requirements shall state the method of measurement in accordance with which the Bills have been prepared;

·2   errors in description or quantity in the Bills shall not vitiate this Contract but any error shall be corrected by the Employer and such correction shall be treated as a Change in the Employer's Requirements;

·3   in any valuation under the Valuation Rules a reference to the rates and prices in the Bills shall be substituted for the references to the values of work set out in the Contract Sum Analysis;

·4   where Fluctuations Option C applies the allocation of items and values in accordance with the Formula Rules shall so far as relevant and applicable be effected by reference to the items and to the rates and prices in the Bills in substitution for the reference to the items and values in the Contract Sum Analysis. In Fluctuations Option C paragraph C·2 after the words "Contract Sum Analysis" the following shall be inserted: ", and the Employer shall provide amplification of any Bills of Quantities included in the Employer's Requirements,".

Valuation of Changes – Contractor's estimates

4   ·1   Section 5 (*Changes*), clauses 2·23 to 2·26 (*Adjustment of Completion Date*) and clauses 4·20 to 4·23 (*Loss and Expense*) shall have effect as modified by the provisions of paragraphs 4·2 to 4·6.

·2   Where compliance with instructions of the Employer under clause 3·9 will in the opinion of the Contractor or of the Employer entail a Valuation under clause 5·2 and/or the making of an adjustment of time in respect of the Relevant Event and/or the ascertainment of direct loss and/or expense under clause 4·20 the Contractor, before such compliance, shall submit to the Employer within 14 days of the date of the relevant instruction (or within such other period as may be agreed or, failing agreement, within such other period as may be reasonable in all the circumstances) estimates, or such of those as are relevant, as referred to in paragraphs 4·3·1 to 4·3·5 unless:

·1   the Employer with the instructions or within 14 days thereafter states in writing that such estimates are not required; or

·2   the Contractor within 10 days of receipt of the instructions raises for himself or on behalf of any sub-contractor reasonable objection to the provision of all or any of such estimates.

·3   The estimates required under paragraph 4·2 shall be in substitution for any Valuation under clause 5·2 and/or any ascertainment under clause 4·20 and shall comprise:

·1   the value of the adjustment to the Contract Sum, supported by all necessary calculations by reference to the values in the Contract Sum Analysis;

·2   the additional resources (if any) required to comply with the instructions;

·3   a method statement for compliance with the instructions;

·4   the length of any extension of time required and the resultant change in the Completion Date;

·5   the amount of any direct loss and/or expense, not included in any other estimate, which results from the regular progress of the Works or any part of them being materially affected by compliance with the instructions under clause 3·9.

·4   Upon submission of the estimates required under paragraph 4·2 the Employer and Contractor shall take all reasonable steps to agree those estimates and upon such agreement those estimates shall be binding on the Employer and Contractor.

·5   If within 10 days of receipt of the Contractor's estimates the Contractor and Employer cannot agree on all or any of the matters therein the Employer:

·1   may instruct compliance with the instruction and that paragraph 4 shall not apply in respect of that instruction; or

·2   may withdraw the instruction.

Where the Employer withdraws the instructions under paragraph 4·5·2 such withdrawal shall be at no cost to the Employer except that where the preparation of the estimates involved the Contractor in any additional design work solely and necessarily carried out for the purpose of preparing his estimates such design work shall be treated as a Change.

·6   If the Contractor is in breach of paragraph 4·2 compliance with the instruction shall be dealt with in accordance with clauses 2·23 to 2·26, 3·9 and 4·20 but any resultant addition to the Contract Sum in respect of such compliance shall not be included in Interim Payments but shall be included in the adjustment of the Contract Sum under clause 4·2. Provided that such addition shall not include any amount in respect of loss of interest or any financing charges in respect of the cost to the Contractor of compliance with the instruction which have been suffered or incurred by him prior to the date of issue of the Final Statement or Employer's Final Statement.

Loss and expense – Contractor's estimates

5   ·1   Clauses 4·20 to 4·23 (*Loss and Expense*) shall have effect as modified by the provisions of paragraphs 5·2 to 5·6.

·2   Where the Contractor pursuant to clause 4·20 is entitled to an amount in respect of direct loss and/or expense to be added to the Contract Sum, he shall (except in respect of direct loss and/or expense dealt with or being dealt with under paragraph 4) on presentation of the next Interim Application for Interim Payment submit to the Employer an estimate of the addition to the Contract Sum which the Contractor requires in respect of such loss and/or expense which he has incurred in the period immediately preceding that for which the Interim Application for Interim Payment has been made.

·3   Following the submission of an estimate under paragraph 5·2 the Contractor shall for so long as he has incurred direct loss and/or expense to which clause 4·20 refers, on presentation of each Interim Application for Interim Payment submit to the Employer an estimate of the addition to the Contract Sum which the Contractor requires in respect of such loss and/or expense which has been incurred by him in the period immediately preceding that for which each Interim Application for Payment is made.

·4 Within 21 days of receipt of any estimate submitted under paragraph 5·2 or 5·3 the Employer may request such information and details as he may reasonably require in support of the Contractor's estimate but within the aforesaid 21 days the Employer shall give to the Contractor notice that:

·1 he accepts the estimate;

·2 he wishes to negotiate on the amount of the addition to the Contract Sum and in default of agreement to refer the issue as a dispute or difference to the Adjudicator in accordance with the provisions of clause 9·2; or

·3 the provisions of clause 4·20 shall apply in respect of the loss and/or expense to which the estimate relates.

If the Employer elects to negotiate pursuant to paragraph 5·4·2 and agreement is not reached, the provisions of clause 4·20 shall apply in respect of the loss and/or expense to which the estimate relates.

·5 Upon acceptance or agreement under paragraph 5·4·1 or 5·4·2 as to the amount of the addition to the Contract Sum such amount shall be added to the Contract Sum and no further additions to the Contract Sum shall be made in respect of the direct loss and/or expense incurred by the Contractor during the period and in respect of the matter set out in clauses 4·20 and 4·21 to which that amount related.

·6 If the Contractor is in breach of paragraphs 5·2 and 5·3 direct loss and/or expense incurred by the Contractor shall be dealt with in accordance with clause 4·20 save that any resultant addition to the Contract Sum shall not be included in Interim Payments but shall be included in the adjustment of the Contract Sum under clause 4·2. Provided that such addition shall not include any amount in respect of loss of interest or financing charges in respect of such direct loss and/or expense which have been suffered or incurred by the Contractor prior to the date of issue of the Final Statement or Employer's Final Statement.

Part 2

Each provision applies unless otherwise stated in the Contract Particulars.

Acceleration Quotation

6 ·1 ·1 If the Employer wishes to investigate the possibility of achieving practical completion before the Completion Date for the Works or a Section he shall invite proposals from the Contractor in that regard (an 'Acceleration Quotation'). The Contractor on receiving such an invitation shall either:

·1 provide an Acceleration Quotation accordingly, identifying the time that can be saved, the amount of the adjustment to the Contract Sum (inclusive of such amounts as are referred to in paragraph 6·1·2) and any other conditions attached; or

·2 explain why it would be impracticable to achieve practical completion earlier than the Completion Date.

·2 The adjustment to the Contract Sum to be specified under paragraph 6·1·1·1 shall include the amount to be paid in respect of any direct loss and/or expense that is not included in any other Confirmed Acceptance or in any ascertainment under clause 4·20 together with a fair and reasonable amount in respect of the cost of preparing the quotation.

·3 The Employer may on or before receipt of the quotation seek revised proposals.

·4 Without affecting his obligations under clauses 2·1 and 2·3, the Contractor shall be under no obligation to accelerate, or take any steps for that purpose, until he receives a Confirmed Acceptance of his Acceleration Quotation under paragraph 6·3.

·2 ·1 Unless otherwise agreed, the Acceleration Quotation shall be submitted in compliance with the invitation not later than 21 days from the later of:

·1 the date of receipt of the invitation; or

  ·2 the date of receipt by the Contractor of information sufficient to enable him to prepare the quotation.

 ·2 The quotation shall remain open for acceptance by the Employer for not less than 7 days from its receipt.

 ·3 The Parties may agree to increase or reduce any of the periods referred to in this paragraph 6; confirmation of such agreement shall be notified to the Contractor by or on behalf of the Employer.

·3 If the Employer wishes to accept an Acceleration Quotation, he shall within the period for acceptance confirm such acceptance by an instruction to the Contractor (a 'Confirmed Acceptance') stating:

 ·1 the adjustment of the Contract Sum (including any amounts referred to in paragraph 6·1·2) to be made for complying with the instruction;

 ·2 the adjustment to the time required by the Contractor for completion of the Works and/or Section and the resultant revised Completion Date(s) (which, where relevant, may be a date earlier than the Date for Completion); and

 ·3 any such conditions as are referred to in paragraph 6·1·1·1.

·4 ·1 If an Acceleration Quotation is not accepted, a fair and reasonable amount shall be added to the Contract Sum in respect of the cost of its preparation provided that it has been prepared on a fair and reasonable basis. Non-acceptance by the Employer of a quotation shall not of itself be evidence that the quotation was not prepared on such a basis.

 ·2 Unless the Employer issues a Confirmed Acceptance, neither the Employer nor the Contractor may use the quotation for any purpose whatsoever.

Collaborative working

7 The Parties shall work with each other and with other project team members in a co-operative and collaborative manner, in good faith and in a spirit of trust and respect. To that end, each shall support collaborative behaviour and address behaviour which is not collaborative.

Health and safety

8 ·1 Without limiting either Party's statutory and/or regulatory duties and responsibilities and/or the specific health and safety requirements of this Contract, the Parties will endeavour to establish and maintain a culture and working environment in which health and safety is of paramount concern to everybody involved with the project.

 ·2 In addition to the specific health and safety requirements of this Contract, the Contractor undertakes to:

  ·1 comply with any and all approved codes of practice produced or promulgated by the Health and Safety Executive and/or the Health and Safety Commission;

  ·2 ensure that all personnel engaged by the Contractor and members of the Contractor's supply chain on site receive appropriate site-specific health and safety induction training and regular refresher training;

  ·3 ensure that all such personnel have access at all times to competent health and safety advice in accordance with regulation 7 of the Management of Health and Safety at Work Regulations 1999; and

  ·4 ensure that there is full and proper health and safety consultation with all such personnel in accordance with the Health and Safety (Consultation with Employees) Regulations 1996.

Cost savings and value improvements

9 ·1 The Contractor is encouraged to propose changes to designs and specifications for the Works and/or to the programme for their execution that may benefit the Employer, whether in the form of a reduction in the cost of the Works or their associated life cycle costs, through

practical completion at a date earlier than the Completion Date or otherwise.

·2   The Contractor shall provide details of his proposed changes, identifying them as suggested under this paragraph 9, together with his assessment of the benefit he believes the Employer may obtain, expressed in financial terms, and a quotation.

·3   Where the Employer wishes to implement a change proposed by the Contractor, the Parties shall negotiate with a view to agreeing its value, the financial benefit and any adjustment to the Completion Date. Upon agreement, the change and the amount of any adjustment of the Contract Sum shall be confirmed in an Employer's instruction, together with the share of the financial benefit to be paid to the Contractor and any adjustment to the Completion Date.

·4   Original proposals by the Contractor under this paragraph 9 may only be instructed in accordance with it, provided always that nothing shall prevent the Employer from utilising other contractors to implement such changes after practical completion of the Works.

Sustainable development and environmental considerations

10   ·1   The Contractor is encouraged to suggest economically viable amendments to the Works which, if instructed as a Change, may result in an improvement in environmental performance in the carrying out of the Works or of the completed Works.

·2   The Contractor shall provide to the Employer all information that he reasonably requests regarding the environmental impact of the supply and use of materials and goods which the Contractor selects.

Performance Indicators and monitoring

11   ·1   The Employer shall monitor and assess the Contractor's performance by reference to any performance indicators stated or identified in the Contract Documents.

·2   The Contractor shall provide to the Employer all information that he may reasonably require to monitor and assess the Contractor's performance against the targets for those performance indicators.

·3   Where the Employer considers that a target for any of those performance indicators may not be met, he may inform the Contractor who shall submit his proposals for improving his performance against that target to the Employer.

Notification and negotiation of disputes

12   With a view to avoidance or early resolution of disputes or differences (subject to Article 7), each Party shall promptly notify the other of any matter that appears likely to give rise to a dispute or difference. The senior executives nominated in the Contract Particulars (or if either is not available, a colleague of similar standing) shall meet as soon as practicable for direct, good faith negotiations to resolve the matter.

Insurance Option A

(New Buildings – All Risks Insurance of the Works by the Contractor)[62]

Contractor to take out and maintain a Joint Names Policy

A·1   The Contractor shall take out and maintain with insurers approved by the Employer a Joint Names Policy for All Risks Insurance with cover no less than that specified in clause 6·8[63] for the full reinstatement value of the Works or (where applicable) Sections (plus the percentage, if any, stated in the Contract Particulars to cover professional fees)[64] and (subject to clause 2·33) shall maintain such Joint Names Policy up to and including the date of issue of the Practical Completion Statement or, if earlier, the date of termination of the Contractor's employment (whether or not the validity of that termination is contested).

The obligation to maintain the Joint Names Policy shall not apply in relation to a Section after the date of issue of the Section Completion Statement for that Section.

Insurance documents – failure by Contractor to insure

A·2   The Contractor shall deposit with the Employer the Joint Names Policy referred to in paragraph A·1, each premium receipt for it and any relevant endorsements of it. If the Contractor defaults in taking out or in maintaining the Joint Names Policy as required by paragraph A·1 (or fails to maintain a policy in accordance with paragraph A·3), the Employer may himself take out and maintain a Joint Names Policy against any risk in respect of which the default has occurred and the amount paid or payable by him in respect of premiums may be deducted by him from any sums due or to become due to the Contractor under this Contract or shall be recoverable from the Contractor as a debt.

Use of Contractor's annual policy – as alternative

A·3   If and so long as the Contractor independently of this Contract maintains an insurance policy which in respect of the Works or Sections:

---

[62]   **Insurance Option A** is applicable to the erection of new buildings where the **Contractor** is required to take out a Joint Names Policy for All Risks Insurance ~~for~~ of the Works and **Insurance Option B** is applicable where the **Employer** has elected to take out ~~such~~ that Joint Names Policy. **Insurance Option C** is for use in the case of alterations of or extensions to existing structures; under it, the **Employer** is required to take out a Joint Names Policy for All Risks Insurance for the Works and also a Joint Names Policy to insure the existing structures and their contents owned by him or for which he is responsible against loss or damage by the Specified Perils. Some Employers (e.g. tenants and homeowners) may not be able readily to obtain the Joint Names cover, in particular that under paragraph C·1. If so, Option C should not be stated to apply and consequential amendments may be necessary. See the Design and Build Contract Guide.

[63]   The risks and costs that All Risks Insurance is required to cover are defined by exclusions. Policies issued by insurers are not standardised; the way in which insurance for these risks is expressed varies and in some cases it may not be possible for insurance to be taken out against certain of the risks required to be covered. In the case of Terrorism Cover, where the extension of cover will involve an additional premium and may in certain situations be difficult to effect, the requirement is now expressly limited to Pool Re Cover or such other cover as is agreed and set out in the Contract Particulars. That extension and any other relevant details require discussion and agreement between the Parties and their insurance advisers prior to entering into the Contract. See the Design and Build Contract Guide. ~~Clause 6·8 defines by exclusions the risks that All Risks Insurance is required to cover: the required cover includes loss or damage caused by or arising from terrorism. Policies issued by insurers are not standardised; the way in which insurance for these risks is expressed varies and in some cases it may not be possible for insurance to be taken out against certain of the risks covered by the definition of All Risks Insurance. In particular the Parties should note the potential difficulty with respect to Terrorism Cover. Obtaining Terrorism Cover, so as to comply with the requirements of Insurance Option A, B or C, will involve an additional premium and may in certain situations be difficult to effect. The exclusion of any element from the All Risks Insurance and its 'buy back' requires discussion between the Parties and their insurance advisers; these are matters that need to be arranged between the Parties and those advisers prior to entering into the Contract. See the Design and Build Contract Guide.~~

[64]   As to reinstatement value, irrecoverable VAT and other costs, see the Design and Build Contract Guide. As respects sub-contractors, note also the provisions of clause 6·9.

·1   provides (inter alia) All Risks Insurance with cover and in amounts no less than those specified in paragraph A·1; and

·2   is a Joint Names Policy,

such policy shall satisfy the Contractor's obligations under paragraph A·1. The Employer may at any reasonable time inspect the policy and premium receipts for it or require that they be sent to the Employer for such inspection. So long as the Contractor, as and when reasonably required to do so, supplies the documentary evidence that the policy is being so maintained, the Contractor shall not be obliged under paragraph A·2 to deposit the policy and premium receipts with the Employer. The annual renewal date of the policy, as supplied by the Contractor, is stated in the Contract Particulars.

Loss or damage, insurance claims and Contractor's obligations

A·4   ·1   If loss or damage affecting any executed work or Site Materials is occasioned by any risk covered by the Joint Names Policy, then, upon its occurrence or later discovery, the Contractor shall forthwith give notice to the Employer of its extent, nature and location.

·2   Subject to clause 6·11·5·2 6·10·4·2 and paragraph A·4·4, the occurrence of such loss or damage shall be disregarded in computing any amounts payable to the Contractor under this Contract.

·3   After any inspection required by the insurers in respect of a claim under the Joint Names Policy has been completed, the Contractor shall with due diligence restore the damaged work, replace or repair any lost or damaged Site Materials, remove and dispose of any debris and proceed with the carrying out and completion of the Works.

·4   The Contractor, for himself and for all his sub-contractors who pursuant to clause 6·9 are recognised as an insured under the Joint Names Policy, shall authorise the insurers to pay all monies from such insurance to the Employer. The Employer shall pay all such amounts to the Contractor (without deduction of Retention and less only the amount stated in paragraph A·4·5) by instalments in accordance with clause 4·14 Alternative B even if Alternative A is applicable to all other payments under this Contract.

·5   The Employer may retain from the monies paid by the insurers the amount properly incurred by the Employer in respect of professional fees up to an amount which shall not exceed the amount of the additional percentage cover for those fees or (if less) the amount paid by insurers in respect of those fees.

·6   In respect of the restoration, replacement or repair of such loss or damage and (when required) the removal and disposal of debris, the Contractor shall not be entitled to any payment other than amounts received under the Joint Names Policy or payable to him under clause 6·11·5·2, where applicable.

Terrorism Cover – premium rate changes

A·5   ·1   If the rate on which the premium is based for Terrorism Cover required under the Joint Names Policy referred to in paragraph A·1 or A·3 is varied at any renewal of the cover, the Contract Sum shall be adjusted by the net amount of the difference between the premium paid by the Contractor and the premium that would have been paid but for the change in the rate.

·2   Where the Employer is a Local Authority, the Employer may, in lieu of any adjustment of the Contract Sum under paragraph A·5·1, instruct the Contractor not to renew the Terrorism Cover under the Joint Names Policy and where he so instructs, the terms of clauses 6·10·4·1 and 6·10·4·2 shall apply from the renewal date if work executed and/or Site Materials suffer physical loss or damage caused by terrorism.

Insurance Option B

(New Buildings – All Risks Insurance of the Works by the Employer)[62]

Employer to take out and maintain a Joint Names Policy

B·1 The Employer shall take out and maintain a Joint Names Policy for All Risks Insurance with cover no less than that specified in clause 6·8[63] for the full reinstatement value of the Works or (where applicable) Sections (plus the percentage, if any, stated in the Contract Particulars to cover professional fees)[64] and (subject to clause 2·33) shall maintain such Joint Names Policy up to and including the date of issue of the Practical Completion Statement or, if earlier, the date of termination of the Contractor's employment (whether or not the validity of that termination is contested).

The obligation to maintain the Joint Names Policy shall not apply in relation to a Section after the date of issue of the Section Completion Statement for that Section.

Evidence of Insurance

B·2 ·1 Except where the Employer is a Local Authority:

·1 the Employer shall, as and when reasonably required by the Contractor, produce documentary evidence and receipts showing that the Joint Names Policy has been taken out and is being maintained; and

·2 if the Employer defaults in taking out or in maintaining the Joint Names Policy, the Contractor may himself take out and maintain a Joint Names Policy against any risk in respect of which the default has occurred and the amount paid or payable by him in respect of the premiums shall be added to the Contract Sum.

·2 Where the Employer is a Local Authority, the Employer shall, as and when reasonably required by the Contractor, produce to the Contractor a copy of the cover certificate issued by the insurer named in the Joint Names Policy certifying that Terrorism Cover is being provided under that policy.

Loss or damage, insurance claims, Contractor's obligations and payment by Employer

B·3 ·1 If loss or damage affecting any executed work or Site Materials is occasioned by any risk covered by the Joint Names Policy, then, upon its occurrence or later discovery, the Contractor shall forthwith give notice to the Employer of its extent, nature and location.

·2 Subject to clause 6·11·5·2 6·10·4·2 and paragraph B·3·5, the occurrence of such loss or damage shall be disregarded in computing any amounts payable to the Contractor under this Contract.

·3 After any inspection required by the insurers in respect of a claim under the Joint Names Policy has been completed, the Contractor shall with due diligence restore the damaged work, replace or repair any lost or damaged Site Materials, remove and dispose of any debris and proceed with the carrying out and completion of the Works.

·4 The Contractor, for himself and for all his sub-contractors who pursuant to clause 6·9 are recognised as an insured under the Joint Names Policy, shall authorise the insurers to pay all monies from such insurance to the Employer.

·5 The restoration, replacement or repair of such loss or damage and (when required) the removal and disposal of debris shall be treated as a Change.

Insurance Option C

(Insurance by the Employer of Existing Structures and Works in or Extensions to them)[62]

Existing structures and contents – Joint Names Policy for Specified Perils

C·1 The Employer shall take out and maintain a Joint Names Policy in respect of the existing structures (which from the Relevant Date shall include any Relevant Part to which clause 2·30 refers) together with the contents thereof owned by him or for which he is responsible, for the full cost of reinstatement[64], repair or replacement of loss or damage due to any of the Specified Perils up to and including the date of issue of the Practical Completion Statement or last Section Completion Statement, or (if earlier) the date of termination of the Contractor's employment (whether or not the validity of that termination is contested). The Contractor shall authorise the insurers to pay all monies from such insurance to the Employer.

The Works – Joint Names Policy for All Risks

C·2 The Employer shall take out and maintain a Joint Names Policy for All Risks Insurance with cover no less than that specified in clause 6·8[63] for the full reinstatement value of the Works or (where applicable) Sections (plus the percentage, if any, stated in the Contract Particulars to cover professional fees)[64] and (subject to clause 2·33) shall maintain such Joint Names Policy up to and including the date of issue of the Practical Completion Statement or, if earlier, the date of termination of the Contractor's employment (whether or not the validity of that termination is contested).

The obligation to maintain the Joint Names Policy under this paragraph C·2 shall not apply in relation to any Section after the date of issue of the Section Completion Statement for that Section.

Evidence of Insurance

C·3 ·1 Except where the Employer is a Local Authority:

·1 the Employer shall, as and when reasonably required by the Contractor, produce documentary evidence and receipts showing that the Joint Names Policies required under paragraphs C·1 and C·2 have been taken out and are being maintained;

·2 if the Employer defaults in taking out or in maintaining either of those Joint Names Policies, the Contractor may himself take out and maintain a Joint Names Policy against any risk in respect of which the default has occurred and for that purpose, in relation to any default under paragraph C·1, shall have such right of entry and inspection as may be required to make a survey and inventory of the existing structures and the relevant contents; and

·3 in the event of any such default, a sum equivalent to the premiums paid or payable by the Contractor pursuant to paragraph C·3·1·2 shall be added to the Contract Sum.

·2 Where the Employer is a Local Authority, the Employer shall, as and when reasonably required by the Contractor, produce to the Contractor copies of the cover certificates issued by the insurers named in the Joint Names Policies under paragraphs C·1 and C·2 which certify that Terrorism Cover is being provided under each policy.

Loss or damage – insurance claims and Contractor's obligations

C·4 ·1 If during the carrying out of the Works there is any loss of or damage of any kind to any of the existing structures or their contents and/or if loss or damage affecting any executed work or Site Materials is occasioned by any of the risks covered by the Joint Names Policy referred to in paragraph C·2 or C·3 then, upon its occurrence or later discovery, the Contractor shall forthwith give notice to the Employer of its extent, nature and location.

·2 Subject to clause 6·11·5·2 6·10·4·2 and paragraph C·4·5·2, the occurrence of such loss or damage to executed work or Site Materials shall be disregarded in computing any amounts payable to the Contractor under this Contract.

·3 The Contractor, for himself and for all his sub-contractors who pursuant to clause 6·9 are recognised as an insured under the Joint Names Policy referred to in paragraph C·2, shall authorise the insurers to pay all monies from the insurances referred to in paragraphs C·2 and C·3 to the Employer.

·4   If there is material loss of or damage to any of the existing structures and it is just and equitable, the Contractor's employment under this Contract may within 28 days of the occurrence of such loss or damage be terminated at the option of either Party by notice given to the other in accordance with clause 1·7·4. If such notice is given:

    ·1   either Party may within 7 days of receiving such a notice (but not thereafter) invoke the dispute resolution procedures that apply under this Contract in order that it may be decided whether the termination is just and equitable; and

    ·2   upon the giving of such notice of termination or, where those dispute resolution procedures have been invoked, upon any final upholding of the notice of termination, the provisions of clauses 8·12·2 to 8·12·5 (except clause 8·12·3·5) shall apply.

·5   If no notice of termination is served under paragraph C·4·4, or if the notice of termination is disputed and is not upheld, then:

    ·1   after any inspection required by the insurers under the Joint Names Policy referred to in paragraph C·2 has been completed, the Contractor shall with due diligence ~~shall~~ restore the damaged work, replace or repair any lost or damaged Site Materials, remove and dispose of any debris and proceed with the carrying out and completion of the Works; and

    ·2   the restoration, replacement or repair of such loss or damage and (when required) the removal and disposal of debris shall be treated as a Change.

Schedule 4 Code of Practice

(Clause 3·13·3)

The purpose of the Code is to assist in the fair and reasonable operation of the requirements of clause 3·13·3.

The Employer and the Contractor should endeavour to agree the amount and method of opening up or testing, but in any case, in issuing his instructions pursuant to that clause, the Employer is required to consider the following criteria:

1   the need in the event of non-compliance to demonstrate at no cost to the Employer either that it is unique and not likely to occur in similar elements of the Works or alternatively, the extent of any similar non-compliance in the Works already constructed or still to be constructed;

2   the need to discover whether any non-compliance in a primary structural element is a failure of workmanship and/or materials such that rigorous testing of similar elements must take place; or, where the non-compliance is in a less significant element, whether it is such as is to be statistically expected and can simply be repaired; or whether the non-compliance indicates an inherent weakness such as can only be found by selective testing, the extent of which must depend upon the importance of any detail concerned;

3   the significance of the non-compliance, having regard to the nature of the work in which it has occurred;

4   the consequence of any similar non-compliance on the safety of the building, its effect on users, adjoining property, the public, and compliance with any Statutory Requirements;

5   the level and standard of supervision and control of the Works by the Contractor;

6   the relevant records of the Contractor and, where relevant, those of any sub-contractor, whether resulting from the supervision and control referred to in paragraph 5 or otherwise;

7   any Codes of Practice or similar advice issued by a responsible body which are applicable to the non-compliant work, materials or goods;

8   any failure by the Contractor to carry out, or to secure the carrying out of, any tests specified in the Employer's Requirements or Contractor's Proposals or in an instruction of the Employer;

9   the reason for the non-compliance, when this has been established;

10   any technical advice that the Contractor has obtained in respect of the non-compliant work, materials or goods;

11   current recognised testing procedures;

12   the practicability of progressive testing in establishing whether any similar non-compliance is reasonably likely;

13   if alternative testing methods are available, the time required for and the consequential costs of such alternative testing methods;

14   any proposals of the Contractor; and

15   any other relevant matters.

Part 1: Third Party Rights for Purchasers and Tenants

('P&T Rights')

1 ·1   The Contractor warrants as at and with effect from practical completion of the Works (or, where there are Sections, practical completion of the relevant Section) that he has carried out the Works or, as the case may be, that Section, in accordance with this Contract. In the event of any breach of this warranty and subject to paragraphs 1·2 and 1·3:

   ·1   the Contractor shall be liable for the reasonable costs of repair, renewal and/or reinstatement of any part or parts of the Works to the extent that the Purchaser or Tenant incurs such costs and/or the Purchaser or Tenant is or becomes liable either directly or by way of financial contribution for such costs; and

   ·2   (if paragraph 1·1·2 is stated in the P&T Rights Particulars to apply) the Contractor shall in addition to the costs referred to in paragraph 1·1·1 be liable for any other losses incurred by the Purchaser or Tenant up to the maximum liability stated in or by the P&T Rights Particulars.

·2   If in or by the P&T Rights Particulars paragraph 1·1·2 is stated or deemed not to apply, the Contractor shall not be liable for any losses incurred by the Purchaser or Tenant other than the costs referred to in paragraph 1·1·1.

·3   The Contractor shall be entitled in any action or proceedings by the Purchaser or Tenant to rely on any term in this Contract and to raise the equivalent rights in defence of liability as he would have against the Employer under this Contract.

·4   The obligations of the Contractor under or pursuant to this paragraph 1 shall not be released or diminished by the appointment of any person by the Purchaser or Tenant to carry out any independent enquiry into any relevant matter.

2   The Contractor further warrants that unless required by this Contract or unless otherwise authorised in writing by the Employer (or, where such authorisation is given orally, confirmed in writing by the Contractor to the Employer), he has not used and will not use materials in the Works other than in accordance with the guidelines contained in the edition of 'Good Practice in Selection of Construction Materials' (Ove Arup & Partners) current at the date of this Contract. In the event of any breach of this warranty the provisions of paragraph 1 shall apply.

3   The Purchaser or Tenant has no authority to issue any direction or instruction to the Contractor in relation to this Contract.

4   The Purchaser or Tenant, insofar as it is the purchaser or tenant of any part(s) of the site, and subject to the Contractor having been paid all sums due and payable under this Contract, shall in respect of such parts have rights and licences in relation to the Contractor's Design Documents in the same terms as those conferred on the Employer by clause 2·38, but subject to similar conditions, limitations and exclusions as apply thereunder to the Employer.

5   Where this Contract so provides, the Contractor warrants that he has and shall maintain Professional Indemnity insurance in and on the terms and for the period referred to in clause 6·12̶1̶1̶ and its related Contract Particulars[65]. The Contractor shall immediately give written notice to the Purchaser or Tenant if such insurance ceases to be available at commercially reasonable rates in order that the Contractor and the Purchaser or Tenant can discuss the means of best protecting their respective positions in the absence of such insurance. As and when i̶t̶ i̶s̶ reasonably requested to do so by the Purchaser or Tenant, the Contractor shall produce for inspection documentary evidence that his Professional Indemnity insurance is being maintained.

---

[65]   For Contractors who do not carry Professional Indemnity insurance, see the Design and Build Contract Guide.

6 P&T Rights may be assigned without the Contractor's consent by a Purchaser or Tenant, by way of absolute legal assignment, to another person (P1) taking an assignment of the Purchaser's or Tenant's interest in the Works and by P1, by way of absolute legal assignment, to another person (P2) taking an assignment of P1's interest in the Works. In such cases the assignment shall only be effective upon written notice of it being given to the Contractor. No further or other assignment of a Purchaser's or Tenant's rights under this Schedule will be permitted and in particular P2 shall not be entitled to assign these rights.

7 Any notice to be given by the Purchaser or Tenant to the Contractor or by the Contractor to the Purchaser or Tenant shall be duly given if delivered by hand or sent by Recorded Signed for or Special Delivery post to the recipient at such address as he may from time to time notify to the sender or (if no such address is then current) his last known principal business address or (where a body corporate) its registered or principal office. Where sent by post in that manner, it shall, subject to proof to the contrary, be deemed to have been received on the second Business Day after the date of posting.

8 No action or proceedings for any breach of P&T Rights shall be commenced against the Contractor after the expiry of the relevant period from the date of practical completion of the Works. Where there are Sections, no action or proceedings shall be commenced against the Contractor in respect of any Section after the expiry of the relevant period from the date of practical completion of such Section. For the purposes of this paragraph, the relevant period shall be:

·1 where this Contract is executed under hand, 6 years; and

·2 where this Contract is executed as a deed, 12 years.

9 For the avoidance of doubt, the Contractor shall have no liability to the Purchaser or Tenant under this Schedule for delay in completion of the Works.

10 This Schedule shall be governed by and construed in accordance with the law of England and the English courts shall have jurisdiction over any dispute or difference between the Contractor and any Purchaser or Tenant which arises out of or in connection with the P&T Rights of that Purchaser or Tenant.

Part 2: Third Party Rights for a Funder

('Funder Rights')

1 The Contractor warrants that he has complied and will continue to comply with this Contract. In the event of any breach of this warranty:

·1 the Contractor shall be entitled in any action or proceedings by the Funder to rely on any term in this Contract and to raise the equivalent rights in defence of liability as he would have against the Employer under this Contract;

·2 the obligations of the Contractor under or pursuant to this paragraph 1 shall not be released or diminished by the appointment of any person by the Funder to carry out any independent enquiry into any relevant matter.

2 The Contractor further warrants that unless required by this Contract or unless otherwise authorised in writing by the Employer (or, where such authorisation is given orally, confirmed in writing by the Contractor to the Employer), he has not used and will not use materials in the Works other than in accordance with the guidelines contained in the edition of 'Good Practice in Selection of Construction Materials' (Ove Arup & Partners) current at the date of this Contract. In the event of any breach of this warranty the provisions of paragraph 1 shall apply.

3 The Funder has no authority to issue any direction or instruction to the Contractor in relation to this Contract unless and until the Funder has given notice under paragraph 5 or 6·4.

4 The Funder has no liability to the Contractor in respect of amounts due under this Contract unless and until the Funder has given notice under paragraph 5 or 6·4.

5 The Contractor agrees that, in the event of the termination of the Finance Agreement by the Funder, the Contractor shall, if so required by written notice given by the Funder and subject to paragraph 7,

accept the instructions of the Funder or its appointee to the exclusion of the Employer in respect of the Works upon the terms and conditions of this Contract. The Employer acknowledges that the Contractor shall be entitled to rely on a notice given to the Contractor by the Funder under this paragraph 5 as conclusive evidence for the purposes of this Contract of the termination of the Finance Agreement by the Funder; and further acknowledges that such acceptance of the instructions of the Funder to the exclusion of the Employer shall not constitute any breach of the Contractor's obligations to the Employer under this Contract.

6 ·1 The Contractor shall not exercise any right of termination of his employment under this Contract without having first:

   ·1 copied to the Funder any notices required by this Contract to be sent to the Employer prior to the Contractor being entitled to give notice under this Contract that his employment under this Contract is terminated; and

   ·2 given to the Funder written notice that he has the right under this Contract forthwith to notify the Employer that his employment under this Contract is terminated.

·2 The Contractor shall not treat this Contract as having been repudiated by the Employer without having first given to the Funder written notice that he intends so to notify the Employer.

·3 The Contractor shall not:

   ·1 issue a notice to the Employer to which paragraph 6·1·2 refers; or

   ·2 notify the Employer that he is treating this Contract as having been repudiated by the Employer as referred to in paragraph 6·2

   before the lapse of 14 days from receipt by the Funder of the notice by the Contractor which the Contractor is required to give under paragraph 6·1·2 or 6·2.

·4 The Funder may, not later than the expiry of the period referred to in paragraph 6·3, require the Contractor by written notice and subject to paragraph 7 to accept the instructions of the Funder or its appointee to the exclusion of the Employer in respect of the Works upon the terms and conditions of this Contract. The Employer acknowledges that the Contractor shall be entitled to rely on a notice given to the Contractor by the Funder under this paragraph 6·4 and that acceptance by the Contractor of the instructions of the Funder to the exclusion of the Employer shall not constitute any breach of the Contractor's obligations to the Employer under this Contract. Provided that, subject to paragraph 7, nothing in this paragraph 6·4 shall relieve the Contractor of any liability he may have to the Employer for any breach by the Contractor of this Contract.

7 It shall be a condition of any notice given by the Funder under paragraph 5 or 6·4 that the Funder or its appointee accepts liability for payment of the sums due and payable to the Contractor under this Contract and for performance of the Employer's obligations including payment of any sums outstanding at the date of such notice. Upon the issue of any notice by the Funder under paragraph 5 or 6·4, this Contract shall continue in full force and effect as if no right of termination of the Contractor's employment under this Contract, nor any right of the Contractor to treat this Contract as having been repudiated by the Employer, had arisen and the Contractor shall be liable to the Funder and its appointee under this Contract in lieu of his liability to the Employer. If any notice given by the Funder under paragraph 5 or 6·4 requires the Contractor to accept the instructions of the Funder's appointee, the Funder shall be liable to the Contractor as guarantor for the payment of all sums from time to time due to the Contractor from the Funder's appointee.

8 Subject to the Contractor having been paid all sums due and payable to under this Contract, the Funder shall in respect of such parts have rights and licences in relation to the Contractor's Design Documents in the same terms as those conferred on the Employer by clause 2·38, but subject to similar conditions, limitations and exclusions as apply thereunder to the Employer.

9 The Contractor warrants that he has and shall maintain Professional Indemnity insurance in and on the terms and for the period referred to in clause 6·12 and its related Contract Particulars[65]. The Contractor shall immediately give written notice to the Funder if such insurance ceases to be available at commercially reasonable rates in order that the Contractor and the Funder can discuss the means of best protecting their respective positions in the absence of such insurance. As and when it is reasonably requested to do so by the Funder or its appointee under paragraph 5 or 6·4, the Contractor shall produce for inspection documentary evidence that his Professional Indemnity insurance is being maintained.

10 The rights contained in this Schedule may be assigned without the Contractor's consent by the

Funder, by way of absolute legal assignment, to another person (P1) providing finance or re-finance in connection with the carrying out of the Works and by P1, by way of absolute legal assignment, to another person (P2) providing finance or re-finance in connection with the carrying out of the Works. In such cases the assignment shall only be effective upon written notice of it being given to the Contractor. No further or other assignment of Funder Rights will be permitted and in particular P2 shall not be entitled to assign these rights.

11   Any notice to be given by the Contractor to the Funder or by the Funder to the Contractor shall be duly given if delivered by hand or sent by Recorded Signed for or Special Delivery post to the recipient at such address as he may from time to time notify to the sender or (if no such address is then current) his last known principal business address or (where a body corporate) its registered or principal office. Where sent by post in that manner, it shall, subject to proof to the contrary, be deemed to have been received on the second Business Day after the date of posting.

12   No action or proceedings for any breach of the rights contained in this Schedule shall be commenced against the Contractor after the expiry of the relevant period from the date of practical completion of the Works. Where there are Sections, no action or proceedings shall be commenced against the Contractor in respect of any Section after the expiry of the relevant period from the date of practical completion of such Section. For the purposes of this paragraph, the relevant period shall be:

   ·1   where this Contract is executed under hand, 6 years; and

   ·2   where this Contract is executed as a deed, 12 years.

13   Notwithstanding the rights contained in this Schedule, the Contractor shall have no liability to the Funder for delay under this Contract unless and until the Funder serves notice pursuant to paragraph 5 or 6·4. For the avoidance of doubt the Contractor shall not be required to pay ~~liquidated~~ damages in respect of the period of delay where the same has been paid to or deducted by the Employer.

14   ·1   This Schedule shall be governed by and construed in accordance with the law of England and subject to paragraph 14·2 the English courts shall have jurisdiction over any dispute or difference between the Contractor and the Funder which arises out of or in connection with this Schedule.

   ·2   Following the giving of any notice by the Funder pursuant to paragraph 5 or 6·4, any dispute or difference which shall arise between the Contractor and the Funder (including any appointee or permitted assignee) shall be subject to the provisions of Article 7 and (where they apply) Article 8 and clauses 9·3 to 9·8.

(Agreed between the JCT and the British Bankers' Association)

Part 1: Advance Payment Bond[66]

1   THE parties to this Bond are:

_____

whose registered office is at _____

_____ ('the Surety'), and

_____

of _____

_____ ('the Employer').

2   The Employer and _____ ('the Contractor')

have agreed to enter into a contract ('the Contract') for building works ('the Works') at _____

_____

3   The Employer has agreed to pay the Contractor the sum of [_____] as an advance payment of sums due to the Contractor under the Contract ('the Advance Payment') for reimbursement by the Surety on the following terms:

    ·1   when the Surety receives a demand from the Employer in accordance with clause 3·2 below the Surety shall repay the Employer the sum demanded up to the amount of the Advance Payment;

    ·2   the Employer shall in making any demand provide to the Surety a completed notice of demand in the form of the **Schedule** attached hereto which shall be accepted as conclusive evidence for all purposes under this Bond. The signatures on any such demand must be authenticated by the Employer's bankers;

    ·3   the Surety shall within 5 Business Days after receiving the demand pay to the Employer the sum so demanded. 'Business Day' means the day (other than a Saturday or a Sunday) on which commercial banks are open for business in London.

4   Payments due under this Bond shall be made notwithstanding any dispute between the Employer and the Contractor and whether or not the Employer and the Contractor are or might be under any liability one to the other. Payment by the Surety under this Bond shall be deemed a valid payment for all purposes of this Bond and shall discharge the Surety from liability to the extent of such payment.

---

[66]   Not applicable where the Employer is a Local Authority.

5 The Surety consents and agrees that the following actions by the Employer may be made and done without notice to or consent of the Surety and without in any way affecting changing or releasing the Surety from its obligations under this Bond and the liability of the Surety hereunder shall not in any way be affected hereby. The actions are:

·1 waiver by the Employer of any of the terms, provisions, conditions, obligations and agreements of the Contractor or any failure to make demand upon or take action against the Contractor;

·2 any modification or changes to the Contract; and/or

·3 the granting of any extensions of time to the Contractor without affecting the terms of clause 7·3 below.

6 The Surety's maximum aggregate liability under this Bond which shall commence on payment of the Advance Payment by the Employer to the Contractor shall be the amount of [_____] which sum shall be reduced by the amount of any reimbursement made by the Contractor to the Employer as advised by the Employer in writing to the Surety.

7 The obligations of the Surety under this Bond shall cease upon whichever is the earliest of:

·1 the date on which the Advance Payment is reduced to nil as certified in writing to the Surety by the Employer;

·2 the date on which the Advance Payment or any balance thereof is repaid to the Employer by the Contractor (as certified in writing to the Surety by the Employer) or by the Surety; and

·3 [*longstop date to be given*],

and any claims hereunder must be received by the Surety in writing on or before such earliest date.

8 This Bond is not transferable or assignable without the prior written consent of the Surety. Such written consent will not be unreasonably withheld.

9 Notwithstanding any other provisions of this Bond nothing in this Bond confers or is intended to confer any right to enforce any of its terms on any person who is not a party to it.

10 This Bond shall be governed and construed in accordance with the laws of England and Wales.

IN WITNESS whereof this Deed of Guarantee has been duly executed and delivered on the date below:

Signed as a Deed by: _____

as the Attorney and on behalf of the Surety: _____

In the presence of:

_____
witness' signature

_____
witness' name

_____
witness' address

_____

Date: _____

Schedule to Advance Payment Bond

(clause 3·2 of the Bond)

Notice of Demand

Date of Notice: _____

Date of Bond: _____

Employer: _____

Surety: _____

The Bond has come into effect.

We hereby demand payment of the sum of

£ _____ (amount in words)
which does not exceed the amount of reimbursement for which the Contractor is in default at the date
of this notice.

Address for payment: _____

_____

This Notice is signed by the following persons who are authorised by the Employer to act for and on
his behalf:

Signed by _____

      Name: _____

      Official Position: _____

Signed by _____

      Name: _____

      Official Position: _____

The above signatures to be authenticated by the Employer's bankers

Part 2: Bond in respect of payment for off-site materials and/or goods

1 THE parties to this Bond are:

_____

whose registered office is at _____

_____

_____ ('the Surety'), and

_____

of _____

_____ ('the Employer').

2 The Employer and _____ ('the Contractor')

have agreed to enter into a contract ('the Contract') for building works ('the Works') at _____

_____

3 Subject to the relevant provisions of the Contract as summarised below but with which the Surety shall not at all be concerned:

·1 the Employer has agreed to include the amount stated as due in Interim Payments (as defined in the Contract) the value of those materials or goods or items pre-fabricated for inclusion in the Works listed by the Employer in a list which has been included as part of the Contract ('the Listed Items'), before their delivery to or adjacent to the Works; and

·2 the Contractor has agreed to insure the Listed Items against loss or damage for their full value under a policy of insurance protecting the interests of the Employer and the Contractor during the period commencing with the transfer of the property in the items to the Contractor until they are delivered to or adjacent to the Works; and

·3 this Bond shall exclusively relate to the amount paid to the Contractor in respect of the Listed Items which have not been delivered to or adjacent to the Works.

4 The Employer shall in making any demand provide to the Surety a Notice of Demand in the form of the **Schedule** attached hereto which shall be accepted as conclusive evidence for all purposes under this Bond. The signatures on any such demand must be authenticated by the Employer's bankers.

5 The Surety shall within 5 Business Days after receiving the demand pay to the Employer the sum so demanded. 'Business Day' means the day (other than a Saturday or a Sunday) on which commercial banks are open for business in London.

6 Payments due under this Bond shall be made notwithstanding any dispute between the Employer and the Contractor and whether or not the Employer and the Contractor are or might be under any liability one to the other. Payment by the Surety under this Bond shall be deemed a valid payment for all purposes of this Bond and shall discharge the Surety from liability to the extent of such payment.

7 The Surety consents and agrees that the following actions by the Employer may be made and done without notice to or consent of the Surety and without in any way affecting changing or releasing the Surety from its obligations under this Bond and the liability of the Surety hereunder shall not in any way be affected hereby. The actions are:

·1 waiver by the Employer of any of the terms, provisions, conditions, obligations and agreements of the Contractor or any failure to make demand upon or take action against the Contractor;

.2   any modification or changes to the Contract; and/or

.3   the granting of an extension of time to the Contractor without affecting the terms of clause 9·2 below.

8   The Surety's maximum aggregate liability under this Bond shall be * [_____].

9   The obligations of the Surety under this Bond shall cease upon whichever is the earlier of:

.1   the date on which all the Listed Items have been delivered to or adjacent to the Works as certified in writing to the Surety by the Employer; or

.2   [*longstop date to be given*],

and any claims hereunder must be received by the Surety in writing on or before such earlier date.

10   The Bond is not transferable or assignable without the prior written consent of the Surety. Such written consent will not be unreasonably withheld.

11   Notwithstanding any other provisions of this Bond nothing in this Bond confers or is intended to confer any right to enforce any of its terms on any person who is not a party to it.

12   This Bond shall be governed and construed in accordance with the laws of England and Wales.

*The value stated in the Contract which the Employer considers will be sufficient to cover him for maximum payments to the Contractor for the Listed Items that will have been made and not delivered to the site at any one time.

IN WITNESS whereof this Deed of Guarantee has been duly executed and delivered on the date below:

Signed as a Deed by: _____

as the Attorney and on behalf of the Surety: _____

In the presence of:

_____
witness' signature

_____
witness' name

_____
witness' address

_____

Date: _____

Schedule to Bond

(clause 4 of the Bond)

Notice of Demand

Date of Notice: _____

Date of Bond: _____

Employer: _____

Surety: _____

We hereby demand payment of the sum of £_____
being the amount in respect of Listed Items included in an Interim Payment(s) which has been duly
made to the Contractor by the Employer but such Listed Items have not been delivered to or adjacent
to the Works.

Address for payment: _____

_____

This Notice is signed by the following persons who are authorised by the Employer to act for and on
his behalf:

Signed by _____

    Name: _____

    Official Position: _____

Signed by _____

    Name: _____

    Official Position: _____

The above signatures to be authenticated by the Employer's bankers

Part 3: Retention Bond[67]

BOND dated the _____ day of _____ 20_____

issued by _____

of _____

_____ ('the Surety')

in favour of _____

of _____

_____ ('the Employer')

1   By a contract ('the Contract') between the Employer and

_____

of _____

_____ ('the Contractor')

the Employer has agreed that he will not exercise his right under the Contract to deduct Retention from amounts included in Interim Payments provided the Contractor has taken out this Bond in favour of the Employer.

2   The Surety is hereby bound to the Employer in the maximum aggregate sum of

_____ (figures and words)

until the Surety is notified by the Employer in writing of the date of issue of the next Interim Payment after practical completion when the maximum aggregate sum shall be reduced by 50 per cent.

3   The Employer shall, on a demand which complies with the requirements in clause 4 below, be entitled to receive from the Surety the sum therein demanded.

4   Any demand by the Employer under clause 3 above shall:

    ·1   be in writing addressed to the Surety at its office at

         _____

         refer to this Bond, and with the signature(s) therein authenticated by the Employer's bankers; and

    ·2   state the amount of the Retention that would have been held by the Employer at the date of the demand had Retention been deductible; and

    ·3   state the amount demanded, which shall not exceed the amount stated pursuant to clause 4·2 above, and identify for which one or more of the following such amount is demanded:

         ·1   the costs actually incurred by the Employer by reason of the failure of the Contractor to comply with the instructions of the Employer under the Contract;

---

[67]   Not applicable where the Employer is a Local Authority.

·2   the insurance premiums paid by the Employer pursuant to the Contract because the Contractor has not taken out and/or not maintained any insurance of the building works which he was required under the Contract to take out and/or maintain;

·3   liquidated and ascertained damages which under the Contract the Contractor is due to pay or allow to the Employer; and be accompanied by a copy of the notice of the Employer which under the Contract he is required to issue and which states that the Contractor has failed to complete the works by the contractual Completion Date;

·4   any expenses or any direct loss and/or damage caused to the Employer as a result of the termination of the Contractor's employment by the Employer;

·5   any costs, other than the amounts referred to in clauses 4·3·1 to 4·3·4 above, which the Employer has actually incurred and which, under the Contract, he is entitled to deduct from monies otherwise due or to become due to the Contractor; and identify his entitlement;

and

·4   incorporate a statement that the Contractor has been given 14 days' written notice of his liability for the amount demanded hereunder by the Employer and that the Contractor has not discharged that liability; and that a copy of this notice has at the same time been sent to the Surety at its office at

_____

Such demand as above shall, for the purposes of this Bond but not further or otherwise, be conclusive evidence (and admissible as such) that the amount demanded is properly due and payable to the Employer by the Contractor.

5   If the Contract is to be assigned or otherwise transferred with the benefit of this Bond, the Employer shall be entitled to assign or transfer this Bond only with the prior written consent of the Surety, such consent not to be unreasonably delayed or withheld.

6   The Surety, in the absence of a prior written demand made, shall be released from its liability under this Bond upon the earliest occurrence of either:

·1   the date of issue under the Contract of the Notice of Completion of Making Good as confirmed by the Employer to the Surety; or

·2   satisfaction of a demand(s) up to the maximum aggregate under the Bond; or

·3   _____ (insert calendar date).

7   Any demand made hereunder must be received by the Surety accompanied by the documents as required by clause 4 above on or before the earliest occurrence as stated above, when this Bond will terminate and become of no further effect whatsoever.

8   Notwithstanding any other provisions of this Bond nothing in this Bond confers or is intended to confer any right to enforce any of its terms on any person who is not a party to it.

9   This Bond shall be governed and construed in accordance with the laws of England and Wales.

IN WITNESS whereof this Deed of Guarantee has been duly executed and delivered on the date below:

Signed as a Deed by: _____

        as the Attorney and on behalf of the Surety: _____

In the presence of:

        _____

        witness' signature

        _____

        witness' name

        _____

        witness' address

        _____

Date: _____

Notes[68]

1   The terms of this Retention Bond have been agreed with the British Bankers' Association and discussed with the Surety Panel of the Association of British Insurers. The JCT understands that a Bond which embodies the terms of this Part 3 of Schedule 6 is, at the proposed Surety's discretion, available to a Contractor where the Employer has incorporated into a building contract in the JCT Design and Build Contract 2005 2011 Edition, optional clause 4·17.

2   In clause 2 the figure to be inserted here is the amount stated in the Contract Particulars pursuant to clause 4·17. It is understood that a Surety will, at additional cost to the Contractor, and which may be subject to other terms and conditions of the Surety, provide for a greater sum than that stated in clause 2 of the Bond if, due to changes, and had Retention been applicable, that amount would have increased. The reduction by 50% of the maximum aggregate sum at the date of issue of the next Interim Payment after practical completion matches a similar reduction had Retention been applicable.

3   The inclusion in the last paragraph of clause 4 of the words "but not further or otherwise" is to make clear that the Contractor would not be prevented by the terms of clause 4 from alleging, under the Contract, that the Contractor was not in breach on any of the matters stated in clauses 4·3·1 to 4·3·5 of the Bond.

     Any demand by the Employer under clause 4 of the Bond must not exceed the costs actually incurred by the Employer and is not to be in excess of the amount stated pursuant to clause 4·2.

4   The Surety will require an actual expiry date to be stated in clause 6·3 of the Bond or (if earlier) a date that is capable of being ascertained on the face of the Bond. Where this is not possible, alternative terms should be discussed with the Surety.

[68]   These Notes will not appear on the Bond issued by the Surety.

Fluctuations Option A

(Contribution, levy and tax fluctuations)

Deemed calculation of Contract Sum – labour

A·1   The Contract Sum shall be deemed to have been calculated in the manner set out below and shall be subject to adjustment in the events specified hereunder.

   ·1   The Contract Sum is based upon the types and rates of contribution, levy and tax payable by a person in his capacity as an employer and which at the Base Date are payable by the Contractor. A type and a rate so payable are in paragraph A·1·2 referred to as a 'tender type' and a 'tender rate'.

   ·2   If any of the tender rates other than a rate of levy payable by virtue of the Industrial Training Act 1982 is increased or decreased, or if a tender type ceases to be payable, or if a new type of contribution, levy or tax which is payable by a person in his capacity as an employer becomes payable after the Base Date, then in any such case the net amount of the difference between what the Contractor actually pays or will pay in respect of:

      ·1   workpeople engaged upon or in connection with the Works either on or adjacent to the site; and

      ·2   workpeople directly employed by the Contractor who are engaged upon the production of materials or goods for use in or in connection with the Works and who operate neither on nor adjacent to the site and to the extent that they are so engaged

       or because of his employment of such workpeople and what he would have paid had the alteration, cessation or new type of contribution, levy or tax not become effective shall, as the case may be, be paid to or allowed by the Contractor.

   ·3   There shall be added to the net amount paid to or allowed by the Contractor under paragraph A·1·2, in respect of each person employed by the Contractor who is engaged upon or in connection with the Works either on or adjacent to the site and who is not within the definition of workpeople in paragraph A·11·3, the same amount as is payable or allowable in respect of a craftsman under paragraph A·1·2 or such proportion of that amount as reflects the time (measured in whole working days) that each such person is so employed.

   ·4   For the purposes of paragraph A·1·3:

      ·1   no period of less than 2 whole working days in any week shall be taken into account and periods of less than a whole working day shall not be aggregated to amount to a whole working day;

      ·2   "the same amount as is payable or allowable in respect of a craftsman" shall refer to the amount in respect of a craftsman employed by the Contractor (or by any sub-contractor under a sub-contract to which paragraph A·3 refers) under the rules or decisions or agreements of the Construction Industry Joint Council or other wage-fixing body and, where those rules or decisions or agreements provide for more than one rate of wage, emolument or other expense for a craftsman, shall refer to the amount in respect of a craftsman employed as aforesaid to whom the highest rate is applicable; and

      ·3   "employed by the Contractor" shall mean an employment to which the Income Tax (Pay As You Earn) Regulations 2003 apply.

   ·5   The Contract Sum is based upon the types and rates of refund of the contributions, levies and taxes payable by a person in his capacity as an employer and upon the types and rates of premium receivable by a person in his capacity as an employer being in each case types and rates which at the Base Date are receivable by the Contractor. Such a type and such a rate are in paragraph A·1·6 referred to as a 'tender type' and a 'tender rate'.

·6   If any of the tender rates is increased or decreased or if a tender type ceases to be payable or if a new type of refund of any contribution, levy or tax payable by a person in his capacity as an employer becomes receivable or if a new type of premium receivable by a person in his capacity as an employer becomes receivable after the Base Date, then in any such case the net amount of the difference between what the Contractor actually receives or will receive in respect of workpeople as referred to in paragraphs A·1·2·1 and A·1·2·2 or because of his employment of such workpeople and what he would have received had the alteration, cessation or new type of refund or premium not become effective shall, as the case may be, be paid to or allowed by the Contractor.

·7   The references in paragraphs A·1·5 and A·1·6 to premiums shall be construed as meaning all payments howsoever they are described which are made under or by virtue of an Act of Parliament to a person in his capacity as an employer and which affect the cost to an employer of having persons in his employment.

·8   Where employer's contributions are payable by the Contractor in respect of workpeople as referred to in paragraphs A·1·2·1 and A·1·2·2 whose employment is contracted-out employment within the meaning of the Pension Schemes Act 1993, the Contractor shall for the purpose of recovery or allowance under this paragraph A·1 be deemed to pay employer's contributions as if that employment were not contracted-out employment.

·9   The references in paragraph A·1 to contributions, levies and taxes shall be construed as meaning all impositions payable by a person in his capacity as an employer howsoever they are described and whoever the recipient which are imposed under or by virtue of an Act of Parliament and which affect the cost to an employer of having persons in his employment.

Deemed calculation of Contract Sum – materials

A·2   The Contract Sum shall be deemed to have been calculated in the manner set out below and shall be subject to adjustment in the events specified hereunder.

·1   The Contract Sum is based upon the types and rates of duty, if any, and tax, if any (other than any VAT which is treated, or is capable of being treated, as input tax by the Contractor), by whomsoever payable which at the Base Date are payable on the import, purchase, sale, appropriation, processing, use or disposal of the materials, goods, electricity, fuels, materials taken from the site as waste or any other solid, liquid or gas necessary for the execution of the Works by virtue of any Act of Parliament. A type and a rate so payable are in paragraph A·2·2 referred to as a 'tender type' and a 'tender rate'.

·2   If, in relation to any materials or goods or any electricity or fuels or materials taken from the site as waste or any other solid, liquid or gas necessary for the execution of the Works including temporary site installations for those Works, a tender rate is increased or decreased or a tender type ceases to be payable or a new type of duty or tax (other than any VAT which is treated, or is capable of being treated, as input tax by the Contractor) becomes payable on the import, purchase, sale, appropriation, processing, use or disposal of any of the above things after the Base Date, then in any such case the net amount of the difference between what the Contractor actually pays in respect of those materials, goods, electricity, fuels, materials taken from the site as waste or any other solid, liquid or gas and what he would have paid in respect of them had the alteration, cessation or imposition not occurred shall, as the case may be, be paid to or allowed by the Contractor. In this paragraph A·2·2 "a new type of duty or tax" includes an additional duty or tax and a duty or tax imposed in regard to any of the above in respect of which no duty or tax whatever was previously payable (other than any VAT which is treated, or is capable of being treated, as input tax by the Contractor).

Sub-contract work – incorporation of provisions to like effect

A·3   ·1   If the Contractor sub-contracts any portion of the Works to a sub-contractor he shall incorporate in the sub-contract provisions to the like effect as the provisions of Fluctuations Option A (excluding this paragraph A·3) including the percentage stated in the Contract Particulars pursuant to paragraph A·12 which are applicable for the purposes of this Contract.

·2   If the price payable under such a sub-contract as referred to in paragraph A·3·1 is increased above or decreased below the price in such sub-contract by reason of the operation of the said incorporated provisions, then the net amount of such increase or decrease shall, as the case may be, be paid to or allowed by the Contractor under this Contract.

Notification by Contractor

A·4 ·1 The Contractor shall notify the Employer of the occurrence of any of the events referred to in such of the following provisions as are applicable for the purposes of this Contract:

  ·1 paragraph A·1·2;

  ·2 paragraph A·1·6;

  ·3 paragraph A·2·2;

  ·4 paragraph A·3·2.

  ·2 Any notification required to be given under paragraph A·4·1 shall be given within a reasonable time after the occurrence of the event to which it relates, and notification in that time shall be a condition precedent to any payment being made to the Contractor in respect of the event in question.

Agreement – Employer and Contractor

A·5 The Employer and the Contractor may agree what shall be deemed for all the purposes of this Contract to be the net amount payable to or allowable by the Contractor in respect of the occurrence of any event such as is referred to in any of the provisions listed in paragraph A·4·1.

Fluctuations added to or deducted from Contract Sum

A·6 Any amount which from time to time becomes payable to or allowable by the Contractor by virtue of paragraphs A·1 and A·2 or paragraph A·3 shall, as the case may be, be added to or deducted from:

  ·1 the Contract Sum; and

  ·2 any amounts payable to the Contractor and which are calculated in accordance with clause 8·12·3·1.

The addition or deduction to which this paragraph A·6 refers shall be subject to the provisions of paragraphs A·7 to A·9·1.

Evidence and computations by Contractor

A·7 As soon as is reasonably practicable the Contractor shall provide such evidence and computations as the Employer may reasonably require to enable the amount payable to or allowable by the Contractor by virtue of paragraphs A·1 and A·2 or paragraph A·3 to be ascertained; and in the case of amounts payable to or allowable by the Contractor under paragraph A·1·3 (or paragraph A·3 for amounts payable to or allowable under the provisions in the sub-contract to the like effect as paragraphs A·1·3 and A·1·4) – employees other than workpeople – such evidence shall include a certificate signed by or on behalf of the Contractor each week certifying the validity of the evidence reasonably required to ascertain such amounts.

No alteration to Contractor's profit

A·8 No addition to or deduction from the Contract Sum made by virtue of paragraph A·6 shall alter in any way the amount of profit of the Contractor included in that Sum.

Position where Contractor in default over completion

A·9 ·1 Subject to the provisions of paragraph A·9·2 no amount shall be added or deducted in the computation of the amount stated as due in an Interim Application for Interim Payment or in the Final Statement or in the Employer's Final Statement in respect of amounts otherwise payable to or allowable by the Contractor by virtue of paragraphs A·1 and A·2 or paragraph A·3 if the event (as referred to in the provisions listed in paragraph A·4·1) in respect of which the payment or allowance would be made occurs after the Completion Date.

  ·2 Paragraph A·9·1 shall not be applied unless:

   ·1 the printed text of clauses 2·23 to 2·26 is unamended and forms part of the Conditions; and

   ·2 the Employer has, in respect of every notification by the Contractor under clause 2·25, fixed or confirmed such Completion Date as he considers to be in accordance with that clause.

Work etc. to which paragraphs A·1 to A·3 not applicable

A·10   Paragraphs A·1 to A·3 shall not apply in respect of:

   ·1   work for which the Contractor is allowed daywork rates under clause 5·5;

   ·2   changes in the rate of VAT charged on the supply of goods or services by the Contractor to the Employer under this Contract.

Definitions for use with Fluctuations Option A

A·11   In Fluctuations Option A:

   ·1   the Base Date means the date stated as such in the Contract Particulars;

   ·2   "materials" and "goods" include timber used in formwork but do not include other consumable stores, plant and machinery;

   ·3   "workpeople" means persons whose rates of wages and other emoluments (including holiday credits) are governed by the rules or decisions or agreements of the Construction Industry Joint Council or some other wage-fixing body for trades associated with the building industry;

   ·4   "wage-fixing body" means a body which lays down recognised terms and conditions of workers;

   ·5   "recognised terms and conditions" means terms and conditions of workers in comparable employment in the trade or industry, or section of trade or industry, in which the employer in question is engaged which have been settled by an agreement or award to which the parties are employers' associations and independent trade unions which represent (generally, or in the district in question, as the case may be) a substantial proportion of the employers and of the workers in the trade, industry or section being workers of the description to which the agreement or award relates.

Percentage addition to fluctuation payments or allowances

A·12   There shall be added to the amount paid to or allowed by the Contractor under:

   ·1   paragraph A·1·2,

   ·2   paragraph A·1·3,

   ·3   paragraph A·1·6,

   ·4   paragraph A·2·2

the percentage stated in the Contract Particulars.

Fluctuations Option B

(Labour and materials cost and tax fluctuations)

Deemed calculation of Contract Sum – labour rates etc.

B·1   The Contract Sum shall be deemed to have been calculated in the manner set out below and shall be subject to adjustment in the events specified hereunder.

·1   The Contract Sum (including the cost of employer's liability insurance and of third party insurance) is based upon the rates of wages and the other emoluments and expenses (including holiday credits) which will be payable by the Contractor to or in respect of:

·1   workpeople engaged upon or in connection with the Works either on or adjacent to the site; and

·2   workpeople directly employed by the Contractor who are engaged upon the production of materials or goods for use in or in connection with the Works and who operate neither on nor adjacent to the site and to the extent that they are so engaged

in accordance with:

·3   the rules or decisions of the Construction Industry Joint Council or other wage-fixing body which will be applicable to the Works and which have been promulgated at the Base Date;

·4   any incentive scheme and/or productivity agreement under the Working Rule Agreement of the Construction Industry Joint Council or provisions on incentive schemes and/or productivity agreements contained in the rules or decisions of some other wage-fixing body; and

·5   the terms of the Building and Civil Engineering Annual and Public Holidays Agreements (or the terms of agreements to similar effect in respect of workpeople whose rates of wages and other emoluments and expenses (including holiday credits) are in accordance with the rules or decisions of a wage-fixing body other than the Construction Industry Joint Council) which will be applicable to the Works and which have been promulgated at the Base Date;

and upon the rates or amounts of any contribution, levy or tax which will be payable by the Contractor in his capacity as an employer in respect of, or calculated by reference to, the rates of wages and other emoluments and expenses (including holiday credits) referred to herein.

·2   If any of the said rates of wages or other emoluments and expenses (including holiday credits) are increased or decreased by reason of any alteration in the said rules, decisions or agreements promulgated after the Base Date, then the net amount of the increase or decrease in wages or other emoluments and expenses (including holiday credits) together with the net amount of any consequential increase or decrease in the cost of employer's liability insurance, of third party insurance and of any contribution, levy or tax payable by a person in his capacity as an employer shall, as the case may be, be paid to or allowed by the Contractor.

·3   There shall be added to the net amount paid to or allowed by the Contractor under paragraph B·1·2, in respect of each person employed by the Contractor who is engaged upon or in connection with the Works either on or adjacent to the site and who is not within the definition of workpeople in paragraph B·12·3, the same amount as is payable or allowable in respect of a craftsman under paragraph B·1·2 or such proportion of that amount as reflects the time (measured in whole working days) that each such person is so employed.

·4   For the purposes of paragraphs B·1·3 and B·2·3:

·1   no period of less than 2 whole working days in any week shall be taken into account and periods of less than a whole working day shall not be aggregated to amount to a whole working day;

·2   "the same amount as is payable or allowable in respect of a craftsman" shall refer to the amount in respect of a craftsman employed by the Contractor (or by any sub-contractor under a sub-contract to which paragraph B·4 refers) under the rules or decisions or agreements of the Construction Industry Joint Council or other wage-fixing body and, where those rules or decisions or agreements provide for more than one rate of wage, emolument or other expense for a craftsman, shall refer to the amount in respect of a craftsman employed as aforesaid to whom the highest rate is applicable; and

.3   "employed by the Contractor" shall mean an employment to which the Income Tax (Pay As You Earn) Regulations 2003 apply.

.5   The Contract Sum is based upon:

.1   the transport charges referred to in a basic transport charges list submitted by the Contractor and attached to the Contractor's Proposals and incurred by the Contractor in respect of workpeople engaged in either of the capacities referred to in paragraphs B·1·1·1 and B·1·1·2; or

.2   the reimbursement of fares which will be reimbursable by the Contractor to workpeople engaged in either of the capacities referred to in paragraphs B·1·1·1 and B·1·1·2 in accordance with the rules or decisions of the Construction Industry Joint Council which will be applicable to the Works and which have been promulgated at the Base Date or, in the case of workpeople so engaged whose rates of wages and other emoluments and expenses are governed by the rules or decisions of some wage-fixing body other than the Construction Industry Joint Council, in accordance with the rules or decisions of such other body which will be applicable and which have been promulgated as aforesaid.

.6   If:

.1   the amount of transport charges referred to in the basic transport charges list is increased or decreased after the Base Date; or

.2   the reimbursement of fares is increased or decreased by reason of any alteration in the said rules or decisions promulgated after the Base Date or by any actual increase or decrease in fares which takes effect after the Base Date,

then the net amount of that increase or decrease shall, as the case may be, be paid to or allowed by the Contractor.

Deemed calculation of Contract Sum – labour levies and taxes

B·2   The Contract Sum shall be deemed to have been calculated in the manner set out below and shall be subject to adjustment in the events specified hereunder.

.1   The Contract Sum is based upon the types and rates of contribution, levy and tax payable by a person in his capacity as an employer and which at the Base Date are payable by the Contractor. A type and a rate so payable are in paragraph B·2·2 referred to as a 'tender type' and a 'tender rate'.

.2   If any of the tender rates other than a rate of levy payable by virtue of the Industrial Training Act 1982 is increased or decreased, or if a tender type ceases to be payable, or if a new type of contribution, levy or tax which is payable by a person in his capacity as an employer becomes payable after the Base Date, then in any such case the net amount of the difference between what the Contractor actually pays or will pay in respect of workpeople as referred to in paragraphs B·1·1·1 and B·1·1·2 or because of his employment of such workpeople and what he would have paid had the alteration, cessation or new type of contribution, levy or tax not become effective shall, as the case may be, be paid to or allowed by the Contractor.

.3   There shall be added to the net amount paid to or allowed by the Contractor under paragraph B·2·2, in respect of each person employed by the Contractor who is engaged upon or in connection with the Works either on or adjacent to the site and who is not within the definition of workpeople in paragraph B·12·3, the same amount as is payable or allowable in respect of a craftsman under paragraph B·2·2 or such proportion of that amount as reflects the time (measured in whole working days) that each such person is so employed. The provisions of paragraph B·1·4 shall apply to this paragraph B·2·3.

.4   The Contract Sum is based upon the types and rates of refund of the contributions, levies and taxes payable by a person in his capacity as an employer and upon the types and rates of premium receivable by a person in his capacity as an employer being in each case types and rates which at the Base Date are receivable by the Contractor. Such a type and such a rate are in paragraph B·2·5 referred to as a 'tender type' and a 'tender rate'.

·5   If any of the tender rates is increased or decreased or if a tender type ceases to be payable or if a new type of refund of any contribution, levy or tax payable by a person in his capacity as an employer becomes receivable or if a new type of premium receivable by a person in his capacity as an employer becomes receivable after the Base Date, then in any such case the net amount of the difference between what the Contractor actually receives or will receive in respect of workpeople as referred to in paragraphs B·1·1·1 and B·1·1·2 or because of his employment of such workpeople and what he would have received had the alteration, cessation or new type of refund or premium not become effective shall, as the case may be, be paid to or allowed by the Contractor.

·6   The references in paragraphs B·2·4 and B·2·5 to premiums shall be construed as meaning all payments howsoever they are described which are made under or by virtue of an Act of Parliament to a person in his capacity as an employer and which affect the cost to an employer of having persons in his employment.

·7   Where employer's contributions are payable by the Contractor in respect of workpeople as referred to in paragraphs B·1·1·1 and B·1·1·2 whose employment is contracted-out employment within the meaning of the Pension Schemes Act 1993, the Contractor shall, subject to the proviso hereto, for the purpose of recovery or allowance under paragraph B·2 be deemed to pay employer's contributions as if that employment were not contracted-out employment; provided that this paragraph B·2·7 shall not apply where the occupational pension scheme, by reference to membership of which the employment of workpeople is contracted-out employment, is established by the rules of the Construction Industry Joint Council or of some other wage-fixing body so that contributions to such occupational pension scheme are within the payment and allowance provisions of paragraph B·1.

·8   The references in paragraphs B·2·1 to B·2·5 and B·2·7 to contributions, levies and taxes shall be construed as meaning all impositions payable by a person in his capacity as an employer howsoever they are described and whoever the recipient which are imposed under or by virtue of an Act of Parliament and which affect the cost to an employer of having persons in his employment.

Deemed calculation of Contract Sum – materials, goods, electricity and fuels

B·3   The Contract Sum shall be deemed to have been calculated in the manner set out below and shall be subject to adjustment in the events specified hereunder.

·1   The Contract Sum is based upon the market prices which were current at the Base Date of the materials, goods, electricity, fuels or any other solid, liquid or gas necessary for the execution of the Works, and upon the duty or tax payable at that date on the disposal of waste from the site.

·2   If after the Base Date the market price of any of the above things increases or decreases, or the duty or tax on the disposal of waste from the site increases or decreases, then the net amount of the difference shall, as the case may be, be paid to or allowed by the Contractor.

·3   The references in paragraphs B·3·1 and B·3·2 to market price(s) shall be construed as including any duty or tax (other than any VAT which is treated, or is capable of being treated, as input tax by the Contractor) by whomsoever payable which is payable under or by virtue of any Act of Parliament on the import, purchase, sale, appropriation, processing, use or disposal of any of the things described in paragraph B·3·1.

Sub-contract work – incorporation of provisions to like effect

B·4 ·1   If the Contractor sub-contracts any portion of the Works to a sub-contractor he shall incorporate in the sub-contract provisions to the like effect as the provisions of Fluctuations Option B (excluding this paragraph B·4) including the percentage stated in the Contract Particulars pursuant to paragraph B·13 which are applicable for the purposes of this Contract.

·2   If the price payable under such a sub-contract as referred to in paragraph B·4·1 is increased above or decreased below the price in such sub-contract by reason of the operation of the said incorporated provisions, then the net amount of such increase or decrease shall, as the case may be, be paid to or allowed by the Contractor under this Contract.

Notification by Contractor

B·5 ·1   The Contractor shall notify the Employer of the occurrence of any of the events referred to in such of the following provisions as are applicable for the purposes of this Contract:

	·1	paragraph B·1·2;
	·2	paragraph B·1·6;
	·3	paragraph B·2·2;
	·4	paragraph B·2·5;
	·5	paragraph B·3·2;
	·6	paragraph B·4·2.

·2 Any notification required to be given under paragraph B·5·1 shall be given within a reasonable time after the occurrence of the event to which it relates, and notification in that time shall be a condition precedent to any payment being made to the Contractor in respect of the event in question.

Agreement – Employer and Contractor

B·6 The Employer and the Contractor may agree what shall be deemed for all the purposes of this Contract to be the net amount payable to or allowable by the Contractor in respect of the occurrence of any event such as is referred to in any of the provisions listed in paragraph B·5·1.

Fluctuations added to or deducted from Contract Sum

B·7 Any amount which from time to time becomes payable to or allowable by the Contractor by virtue of paragraphs B·1 to B·3 or paragraph B·4 shall, as the case may be, be added to or deducted from:

·1 the Contract Sum; and

·2 any amounts payable to the Contractor and which are calculated in accordance with clause 8·12·3·1.

The addition or deduction to which paragraph B·7 refers shall be subject to the provisions of paragraphs B·8 to B·10·1.

Evidence and computations by Contractor

B·8 As soon as is reasonably practicable the Contractor shall provide such evidence and computations as the Employer may reasonably require to enable the amount payable to or allowable by the Contractor by virtue of paragraphs B·1 to B·3 or paragraph B·4 to be ascertained; and in the case of amounts payable to or allowable by the Contractor under paragraph B·1·3 (or paragraph B·4 for amounts payable to or allowable under the provisions in the sub-contract to the like effect as paragraphs B·1·3 and B·1·4) – employees other than workpeople – such evidence shall include a certificate signed by or on behalf of the Contractor each week certifying the validity of the evidence reasonably required to ascertain such amounts.

No alteration to Contractor's profit

B·9 No addition to or deduction from the Contract Sum made by virtue of paragraph B·7 shall alter in any way the amount of profit of the Contractor included in that Sum.

Position where Contractor in default over completion

B·10 ·1 Subject to the provisions of paragraph B·10·2 no amount shall be added or deducted in the computation of the amount stated as due in an Interim Application for Interim Payment or in the Final Statement or in the Employer's Final Statement in respect of amounts otherwise payable to or allowable by the Contractor by virtue of paragraphs B·1 to B·3 or paragraph B·4 if the event (as referred to in the provisions listed in paragraph B·5·1) in respect of which the payment or allowance would be made occurs after the Completion Date.

·2 Paragraph B·10·1 shall not be applied unless:

·1 the printed text of clauses 2·23 to 2·26 is unamended and forms part of the Conditions; and

·2 the Employer has, in respect of every notification by the Contractor under clause 2·25, fixed or confirmed such Completion Date as he considers to be in accordance with that clause.

Work etc. to which paragraphs B·1 to B·4 not applicable

B·11   Paragraphs B·1 to B·4 shall not apply in respect of:

    ·1   work for which the Contractor is allowed daywork rates under clause 5·5;

    ·2   changes in the rate of VAT charged on the supply of goods or services by the Contractor to the Employer under this Contract.

Definitions for use with Fluctuations Option B

B·12   In Fluctuations Option B:

    ·1   the Base Date means the date stated as such in the Contract Particulars;

    ·2   "materials" and "goods" include timber used in formwork but do not include other consumable stores, plant and machinery;

    ·3   "workpeople" means persons whose rates of wages and other emoluments (including holiday credits) are governed by the rules or decisions or agreements of the Construction Industry Joint Council or some other wage-fixing body for trades associated with the building industry;

    ·4   "wage-fixing body" means a body which lays down recognised terms and conditions of workers;

    ·5   "recognised terms and conditions" means terms and conditions of workers in comparable employment in the trade or industry, or section of trade or industry, in which the employer in question is engaged which have been settled by an agreement or award to which the parties are employers' associations and independent trade unions which represent (generally, or in the district in question, as the case may be) a substantial proportion of the employers and of the workers in the trade, industry or section being workers of the description to which the agreement or award relates.

Percentage addition to fluctuation payments or allowances

B·13   There shall be added to the amount paid to or allowed by the Contractor under:

    ·1   paragraph B·1·2,

    ·2   paragraph B·1·3,

    ·3   paragraph B·1·6,

    ·4   paragraph B·2·2,

    ·5   paragraph B·2·5,

    ·6   paragraph B·3·2

the percentage stated in the Contract Particulars.

Fluctuations Option C

(Formula adjustment)

Adjustment of Contract Sum – Formula Rules

C·1   ·1   ·1   The Contract Sum shall be adjusted in accordance with the provisions of Fluctuations Option C and the Formula Rules current at the Base Date issued for use with Fluctuations Option C by the JCT ('the Formula Rules').

               ·2   Any adjustment under Fluctuations Option C shall be to sums exclusive of VAT and nothing in Fluctuations Option C shall affect in any way the operation of clause 4·4.

      ·2   The Definitions in rule 3 of the Formula Rules shall apply to Fluctuations Option C.

      ·3   The adjustment referred to in Fluctuations Option C shall be effected (after taking into account any Non-Adjustable Element[69]) in all applications for payment issued under the provisions of the Conditions.

      ·4   If any correction of amounts of adjustment under Fluctuations Option C included in previous payments is required following any operation of rule 5 of the Formula Rules, such correction shall be given effect in the next payment to be made.

Interim Application ~~for Interim Payment~~ – statement of allocation of values

C·2   The Contractor shall provide any amplification of the Contract Sum Analysis necessary to ensure the allocation of items and values in accordance with the Formula Rules. When making an Interim Application ~~for Interim Payment~~ under clause 4·89 the Contractor shall include a statement of the allocation of the values and the amount of their adjustment in accordance with Fluctuations Option C and the Formula Rules.

Fluctuations – articles manufactured outside the United Kingdom

C·3   For any article to which rule 4(ii) of the Formula Rules applies the Contractor shall insert in a list attached to the Contractor's Proposals the market price of the article in sterling (that is the price delivered to the site) current at the Base Date. If after that date the market price of the article inserted in that list increases or decreases then the net amount of the difference between the cost of purchasing at the market price inserted in such list and the market price payable by the Contractor and current when the article is bought shall, as the case may be, be paid to or allowed by the Contractor. The reference to market price in this paragraph C·3 shall be construed as including any duty or tax (other than any VAT which is treated, or is capable of being treated, as input tax by the Contractor) by whomsoever payable under or by virtue of any Act of Parliament on the import, purchase, sale, appropriation or use of the article specified as aforesaid.

Power to agree – Employer and Contractor

C·4   The Employer and the Contractor may agree any alteration to the methods and procedures for ascertaining the amount of formula adjustment to be made under Fluctuations Option C, and the amounts ascertained after the operation of such agreement shall be deemed for all the purposes of this Contract to be the amount of formula adjustment payable to or allowable by the Contractor in respect of the provisions of Fluctuations Option C. Provided always that no alteration to the methods and procedures shall be agreed unless it is reasonably expected that the amount of formula adjustment so ascertained will be the same or approximately the same as that ascertained in accordance with Part I or Part II of Section 2 of the Formula Rules whichever Part is stated to be applicable in the Employer's Requirements or the Contractor's Proposals.

Position where Monthly Bulletins are delayed, etc.

C·5   ·1   If at any time prior to the due date for the final payment under clause 4·12·5 ~~Final Statement becoming conclusive under clause 4·12·4 or prior to the Employer's Final Statement becoming conclusive under clause 4·12·7~~ formula adjustment is not possible because of delay in, or cessation of, the publication of the Monthly Bulletins, adjustment of the Contract Sum shall be made in each Interim Application ~~for Interim Payment~~ during such period of delay on a

---

[69]   Applies to Local Authorities only.

fair and reasonable basis.

·2   If publication of the Monthly Bulletins is recommenced at any time prior to the ~~due date for the final payment~~ Final Statement becoming conclusive under clause 4·12·4 or prior to the Employer's Final Statement becoming conclusive under clause 4·12·7, the provisions of Fluctuations Option C and the Formula Rules shall apply for each Valuation Period as if no delay or cessation had occurred and the adjustment under Fluctuations Option C and the Formula Rules shall be substituted for any adjustment under paragraph C·5·1.

·3   During any such period of delay or cessation the Contractor and the Employer shall operate such parts of Fluctuations Option C and the Formula Rules as will enable the amount of formula adjustment due to be readily calculated upon recommencement of publication of the Monthly Bulletins.

Formula adjustment – failure to complete

C·6   ·1   ·1   If the Contractor fails to complete the Works by the Completion Date, formula adjustment of the Contract Sum under Fluctuations Option C shall be effected in all statements given under paragraph C·2 with Interim Applications ~~for Interim Payments~~ issued after the Completion Date by reference to the Index Numbers applicable to the Valuation Period in which the Completion Date falls.

           ·2   If for any reason the adjustment included in the amount of any Interim Application ~~for Interim Payment~~ which is or has been made after the Completion Date is not in accordance with paragraph C·6·1·1, such adjustment shall be corrected to comply with that paragraph.

     ·2   Paragraph C·6·1 shall not be applied unless:

           ·1   the printed text of clauses 2·23 to 2·26 is unamended and forms part of the Conditions; and

           ·2   the Employer has, in respect of every notification by the Contractor under clause 2·25, fixed or confirmed such Completion Date as he considers to be in accordance with that clause.